YET

EMBRACING GOD'S FAITHFULNESS IN THE MIDST OF GRIEF

TYLER QUILLET

Foreword by Dr. Thom S. Rainer

Yet
© 2020 Tyler Quillet

ISBN 978-0-578-71478-3

Dire Dawa Publishing
Nashville, TN

Printed in the United States of America

To Cathie

Together, we have grieved much loss. Yet, our hope has never wavered. Together. We have done this together, and there's nobody I'd rather have by my side for the highest of highs and lowest of lows that this life has to offer. I love you.

CONTENTS

Foreword 9

Introduction.. 13

1) The Lament: How? 25

2) Your Grieving Heart 39

3) Choosing to Live in the "Yet" 53

4) Clinging to Hope 75

5) He's Faithful & Present 103

6) From Peace to Rejoicing....................... 119

7) Moving Forward in the Yet 139

Endnotes.. 161

*At every moment of the lengthening grief,
we turn to him, not away from him. And
therefore, the length of it is a way of showing
him to be ever-present, enduringly sufficient.* [1]
-JOHN PIPER

FOREWORD

I remember the young man whose father died at a relatively young age.

I remember the young man's pain, questions, and struggles.

I remember his grief.

The young man tried to make sense of this death. His dad was his confidant, best friend, and hero. Death had seemingly jerked his dad away from him before he could realize what happened.

You see, I remember that young man because I am he.

If someone like Tyler Quillet had come alongside me and shared with me his guiding principle for grief, I would have dealt with my struggles so much better. I wish someone had whispered this sentence in my ears. Read Tyler's words carefully. Read his words prayerfully:

Christians should be able to go from "I have Jesus, but I'm completely overwhelmed by grief" to "I have grief, but I am completely overwhelmed by Jesus."

Wow.

It's a book with a simple title: Yet. But it's a book with a profound message.

Tyler Quillet knows grief all too well. He has experienced the personal loss of loved ones many times. He has known the pain of grief again and again. He also officiated or served in over 100 funerals. He has walked alongside many who were grieving.

Tyler has been driven to Lamentations 3:17-25 many times. The prophet Jeremiah expresses his own deep and profound grief. All the words are powerful, but read these two poignant sentences from the prophet: " Peace has been stripped from me, and I have forgotten what prosperity is. I will never forget this awful time as I grieve over my loss."

Yet Tyler remembers that Jeremiah does not grieve without hope, citing Lamentations 3:21-24: "Yet I still dare to hope when I remember this: The faithful love of the Lord never ends! His mercies never cease. Great is his faithfulness; his mercies begin afresh each morning. I say to myself, 'The Lord is my inheritance; therefore I will hope in him!'"

There it is. There is that little three-letter transition word: Yet.

Yet, I will dare to hope in him. In the midst of the deepest grief, we have the Lord whose mercy is infinitely deeper.

This book can and should be a powerful and poignant reminder for those experiencing grief. God does not immediately take the grief away, but He does provide the mercy we so desperately need in these times of struggle. We are reminded that it is OK to grieve. But we are not to be so focused on our loss that we forget God, the One who will sustain us and walk with us on this painful journey.

Thank you, Tyler, for writing this book. Even more, thank you for reminding us afresh of the reality of grief *and* the reality of the mercies of God in the midst of the grief.

"Yet I still dare to hope when I remember this: The faithful love of the Lord never ends! His mercies never cease. Great is his faithfulness; his mercies begin afresh each morning."

Amen and amen.

Thom S. Rainer
Founder and CEO, Church Answers
Author, *Anatomy of a Revived Church*

INTRODUCTION

Friend, I am so sorry. I am so sorry for the loss of your loved one(s). I am sorry for the neverending tears you've cried. I am sorry for the deep hurt you have felt. I am sorry for the loneliness you've experienced. I am sorry for the sleepless nights, anxiety, lack of peace, and the deep sense of agony that you have encountered. My heart aches for you and your loved ones who continue to mourn deeply. While I hurt for you, I also hope for you.

No matter how long it has been since your loved one(s) passed away, you will never forget this awful time. It has been truly awful, hasn't it? Probably worse than you could have ever imagined. And yet, as you continue to grieve (and that's a good thing...keep grieving), it's possible to do so with much peace. Christian, you can grieve while filled with hope. As Christians, we need permission to do both. For some reason, it feels wrong to grieve, doesn't it? Whether it's our own hearts or someone else telling us that if we grieve, then we must not be trusting God. That's just not true. As you continue to trust the Lord, allow your heart to grieve over the person you love so dearly who is no longer here with you. We'll talk often in the pages ahead about living in grief and hope all at once. That's an OK place to be, as long as we've got our eyes fixed tightly on the Father. As we do this, as we cling to Him with the hope only He gives, we can still hurt deeply inside because of those who are gone that we so dearly love.

As we navigate this grief journey together, I want to point you to the hope there is in Jesus, even when all feels hopeless. He is faithful, full of mercy, and present with you. Because of this, you and I can move forward in the midst of our grief with confident hope in Him.

The premise of this book has been on my heart for years. It comes out of Lamentations 3:17-24. This is a text that I've shared often with grieving folks as a pastor. It has had such an impact on my own heart, that I've wanted everyone to grab hold of these truths in their own grief! Let me share with you a portion of it and we'll go more in-depth as we move along throughout the pages ahead.

> *Peace has been stripped away....Everything I had hoped for from the Lord is lost! The thought of my suffering...is bitter beyond words. I will never forget this awful time, as I grieve over my loss. Yet I still dare to hope when I remember this: The faithful love of the Lord never ends! His mercies never cease. Great is his faithfulness; his mercies begin afresh each morning. I say to myself, "The Lord is my inheritance; therefore, I will hope in him!*
> **- Lamentations 3:17-24 (NLT)** [2]

In your grief, are you feeling like your peace has been stripped away? Do you sense that your hopes and dreams have been lost, both personally and for your loved one who is gone? Has the idea of your suffering brought your heart a degree of bitterness? No matter how long it has been since your loved one passed away, you haven't forgotten the awfulness of it, have you?

"YET"

This is a BIG word. It's a dramatic turn in the posture of our hearts. We start with the reality of the situation that is being faced. Grief has stripped the heart of peace, there is bitter suffering that you cannot seem to shake. YET (although those things are true), there is a greater truth going on here. God is faithful. His love never ends. His mercies never cease, and those mercies are even new for you and I each morning. So, because of these incredible truths, we can hope in Him! This unbelievable and unshakable hope is what we'll dig into in the pages ahead.

Before we really get going, I want you to know that I've been there. I don't know your story and I won't pretend to. ALL of our grief stories are different and each of our responses to those losses are different. For me, both personally and professionally, I've experienced considerable loss. I've grieved heavily as a pastor, friend, family member, and father. I'll never forget the heartbreaking exposures to loss that I've encountered over the years. I want to give you a glimpse into my heart, where I've been, and what kinds of grief I continue to navigate through. I'm no expert on grief and I'm certainly not comparing my grief experience to yours or anyone else's.

However, as I've journeyed alongside many hurting people and walked my own extensive road of grief, I feel that I've learned and grown much because of it. I'd love to share with you the truths I've learned about God and His incredible presence with and faithfulness to those who trust Him.

So, what does my grief journey look like? It has been a difficult journey, to say the least. Pastoring at the church I grew up in meant a lot of really close relationships with people I had known my entire life. On top of that, my wife Cathie and I have lost a number of close friends and family members in ways that were completely unexpected and still leave us shaking our heads in disbelief. It has been a tough road. This is not the complete list of those I've grieved losing, but as I ponder those losses that have affected my heart most, these come to mind.

When I was in middle school, my uncle Scott was killed in a horrific accident that occurred while cutting down a tree. We kids sat at home all day waiting with other family members for some sort of good news while the rest of the family was at the hospital. Forever burned in my brain is the image of my dad getting out of the car and walking up our front steps toward the house that night. The look on his face as he entered the house was all I needed to see to know that he had lost his brother and best friend and that our lives were suddenly turned upside down. This was my first real grief experience. The first person I'd ever lost that I loved deeply. I'll never forget this awful time...

On Christmas Eve, 2007, we were in San Diego, doing the holidays with Cathie's family. Late that evening, I got a call that still today feels like a bad dream. My grandparent's neighbors (who would years later become our neighbors and dear friends) had a high school-aged daughter, Hollis. Hollis was out with her boyfriend's family for a family Christmas. On the way home, someone pulled out in front of them. Hollis was killed. Her boyfriend Elliot's dad, David, was killed. Elliot's brother, Brock, was paralyzed. Our community was wrecked with grief on Christmas. You may have seen this story on ESPN over the years. Elliot went on to play football at the University of Michigan. Brock was given a one percent chance of walking. Brock walked again. He was in a men's bible study with me a few years later and his story has been an incredible inspiration to me and so many others! My heart continues to break for Hollis' parents, Fred & Hope, and her sister's, McKalyn & Maddie. I'll share more about them later. They're a true model of clinging to Jesus and finding hope in Him in the midst of grief. This was a horrific tragedy that still leaves me shaking my head in disbelief. I'll never forget this awful time...

John was a friend, mentor, my volunteer youth leader, and my favorite Canadian (no offense to the other Canadians in my life). John battled cancer for years and his trust in Christ was absolutely unwavering. John eventually entered hospice care, where Cathie and I had the gut-wrenching privilege of sitting through the middle of the night with John, his wife, and two children as he took his final breath on this earth and was ushered into the presence of Jesus. I'll never forget this awful time...

Randy was the father of a student in my youth group.

He took his own life, leaving behind a wife and 3 teen / college-aged children. This man was heavily involved in our church. I had just baptized his son 3 months earlier. Our pastoral staff sat in their home, consoling this completely broken family for hours upon hours. This is a day in ministry that I think of often, and it still brings me to a place of overwhelming sadness. I'll never forget this awful time...

Two students from my Junior High youth group went to a friend's house early one morning so they could all walk to school together. The father of that child was gone and he left a shotgun laying out. One of the boys in my group picked up the gun, thinking it was unloaded, pointed it at the other boy in my group as a "joke", and accidentally discharged the shotgun at point-blank range. 13-year-old Michael died that morning. It's a regular occurrence that I think of all that I witnessed that day, and I am still shaken to the core by it. One boy in jail, another lost his life. A school and youth group full of confused, broken, and hurting teens. A family wracked with grief. I'll never forget this awful time...

LJ came from a tough background. He loved Jesus, but because of his home life, he needed much direction. I spent more time with LJ than any kid in my early years of youth ministry. I discipled him, did regular coffee get-togethers before school, and took him along with me to do pastoral visits and various other everyday errands, even as he went on to high school. He even helped me disciple the young man who accidentally shot and killed his friend in the previous story. LJ began getting into some trouble, much that I was unaware of because he was ashamed to tell me. Then,

I got the call. In a moment of desperation that I still cannot fathom, LJ hung himself. He was 16. I felt like I lost a child of my own that day. I'll never forget this awful time...

Ava was a 7-year-old little girl with a smile that would melt your heart. Ava had the flu and got so sick that her parents took her to the hospital, where she passed away suddenly. I've never felt so overwhelmed and heartbroken at any funeral I've ever led. Seeing that little casket, having small children of my own. Sitting with completely overwhelmed parents who cannot begin to fathom what they are experiencing. Holding little brothers and sisters who have just lost their sibling and best friend. Ava's passing still gets to me. I have flashbacks about that week and/or her funeral on a regular basis. I'll share more later about Ava and God's redemptive power in and through her family. I'll never forget this awful time...

Louie was a mentor, friend, pastor in the town I grew up and pastored in, and my greatest encourager and cheer-leader. Louie was an amazing friend. He was with me when I first felt a call to ministry. He pushed me, challenged me, and loved the heck out of me (and everyone else in his life, for that matter). Even after we moved from Ohio to Tennessee, Louie was always faithful to stay in touch, call-ing on a regular basis to check-in. There is nobody in my life who championed me more than he. Louie battled a lot of health issues over the years. He went to sleep one night and never woke up. I miss his constant encouragement, his bear claw-like hand on my shoulder as he prayed for me, his hysterical wheezing laugh, and his deep love for Jesus. I'll never forget this awful time...

When Cathie and I got married, we had big dreams and expectations about what our family would one-day look like. As we began to try and start our family, we found that it would be incredibly difficult. It took quite a while, but we eventually became expectant parents! We were overwhelmed with joy! The day I heard our first child's heartbeat was one of the greatest moments of my life. It wasn't long after that we went to the hospital with the feeling that something just wasn't right. As the nurse performed the ultrasound, I was ready to hear that heartbeat again, but it never came. All the nurse could utter was a soft, "I'm sorry," and she walked out of the room so we could have time alone to grieve. We were completely broken. We would end up experiencing this same joy that resulted in grief three more times. I understand that the grief of miscarriage is different from losing someone you've known and loved. If you've ever experienced miscarriage, you know the grief is real. It's different, certainly, but it's VERY real. I'll never forget this awful time...

In the fall of 2016, Cathie's mom, Sandi, passed away. It's still hard for us. Sandi had battled and overcome breast cancer 12 years prior. It returned, metastasized to various parts of the body, and it was aggressive. We got one year with her after the diagnosis. It was a hard year for her physically, but she made the absolute most out of it. She was an amazing woman, full of spunk, and she loved Jesus! She lived life to the full and we know she is with her Savior. It still hurts though. We miss her so much and Cathie daily grieves her mom's passing. On a regular basis, our oldest son Cylas says he's sad because he misses his Nana. It's so hard to do everyday life without someone you are used to doing virtually every single day with, even from a distance. Losing someone this close makes for heartache that never really goes away. I'll never forget this awful time...

I'd be remiss to not mention so many others who I've grieved their passing and walked alongside their families in my many years of full-time ministry. I can't mention them all by name, but over the years, I have led, assisted in, or planned over 100 funerals. This doesn't include all of those in our former church family who we sat and journeyed with as they grieved the loss of a loved one. There are so many grieving hearts that I've walked alongside over these years. I've seen grief drive people away from Jesus and I've seen the beauty of the gospel use grief to drive people into a deeper, or even new trust in Jesus. And this is why I write. Because there's hope to be found as we grieve. I'm excited to walk this difficult but blessed journey through grief with you as we find and fully embrace together the hope that we have in Christ Jesus!

In the coming chapters, we'll cover everything from your own grief, what to do with your emotions, God's goodness through it, and how we move forward filled with hope. You'll be given numerous opportunities in each chapter to respond by writing or simply pondering a question, if you choose. Here's a quick overview of what's to come:

- In chapter one, we'll be introduced to the book of Lamentations and the "grief roadmap" Jeremiah gives us as we navigate the "how" questions of our own grief.

- In chapter two, we'll discuss the grief you are personally feeling and experiencing. What does the state of your grief look like right now and what are you doing with it?

- In chapter three, we'll dig more deeply into Lamentations 3, where we see Jeremiah go from overwhelmed by grief to overwhelmed by God's goodness. His grief didn't go away, but he chose to live in hope. And, so can you!

- In chapter four, we'll discuss that hope, how to find it, who provides it, and what it looks like to live life with a broken heart that continues to hope in the Lord.

- In chapter five, we'll focus on just how faithful and present God is. That's a truth we know well, but we tend to forget it when grieving.

- In chapter six, we'll see that it's not just peace that we're hoping for, but for that peace to lead us to rejoice in the Lord again. What does it look like for your heart to rejoice again? It's possible, and God will do that work in and through you.

- In chapter seven, our goal is to help us move forward in peace, in hope, and in rejoicing. Moving forward means that in the midst of my grief, I can be in community again, I can worship again, I can serve again, live on mission again, and be the hands and feet of Jesus again. It's difficult to go back to daily life in Jesus after a shake-up like this, but it's necessary, it's good, and it's what God has called us to do. Maybe you aren't there yet, but what might it look like for you to point grieving people to Jesus because of your testimony of His faithfulness in the midst of your own grief story?

There are some amazing things ahead in this book for you. There are some incredible truths that you'll cling to. There are some hard truths that you'll not want to admit or acknowledge. There are some new truths that you've maybe never heard before. May this book be a small source of healing along the way in your grief journey. This may seem crazy to hear, but as my brother or sister in Christ, I want you to know that I love you, I care deeply for you, and my heart is broken for you. I don't know your specific story (I'd love to hear it someday), and I won't pretend to. But I do know that God is incredibly faithful and He will prove to be all that you need at this time.

So, as we begin, let's address the elephant in the room. This grief you are facing is hard. What you are dealing with is a daily punch to the gut. Peace is lacking, anxiety is thriving, and hopelessness can often be the driving force of each day. Bitterness creeps up out of nowhere. The daily suffering can be all-consuming. It feels like normalcy is forever in the past and this millstone of grief will continue to drag you down as long as you live. You'll never forget this awful time as you grieve over your loss.

Yet...

CHAPTER 1

THE LAMENT: HOW?

"How is this happening?"
"How is this possible?"
"How did we get here?"
"How could God allow this?"
"How am I ever going to move forward?"
"How will I ever find peace again?"

You've most definitely thought to yourself or asked someone at least one of these questions. Probably more. Maybe even all of them. As your heart grieves, it's impossible NOT to simply ask, *"how....?"* It's the staring-off into space with tear-filled eyes, slowly shaking your head back and forth, semi-unaware of your surroundings, and wondering if this is some sort of nightmare you are trapped in.

Too many times in my life, either myself or someone I was sitting with received the news that their loved one was gone. I've taken the long, cold trek into the hospital basement with a family to identify their son. I've sat with parents who learned at age 5, their son was diagnosed with cancer, and I stood with them in a circle around him as he took his final breaths 9 years later. I've waited for hours in ER waiting rooms with anxiety-ridden family members, only to have the doctor come out with that look...we all know that look. I've sat in a living room, holding the hand of one whose life slowly faded with their family surrounding them. I've been called by police, asking me to hurry to the scene to be with the family who has been given the news of their son's passing. I've knocked on the front door to inform a family that their loved one was gone. I've shown up at a home at 3 a.m. to sit with a wife whose husband died in his sleep. I've walked into ER rooms that looked like a warzone, only to see a deceased friend with hysterical loved ones in their initial moments of grief and despair. I've stood next to my grandfather, rubbing his shoulder and praying with my family surrounding him and I've stood with strangers who had simply begged to have a pastor present as their loved one died. I've been in emergency rooms, bedrooms, hospice rooms, and everywhere in between, experiencing first-hand so many people passing away and so many families entering into a state of grief they've never experienced before. As I stated earlier, these moments truly feel like a nightmare. You can never be prepared for them, but if you are reading this right now, you know that these moments happen. You've lived it.

From a parent screaming, "No, no, no....." to a child sitting in utter shock, unable to muster a word. It's at this moment that the grief begins and with it comes this sort of "shell-shock" moment that can last quite some time in the grief process.

You may be reading this still feeling that state of shock, unable to shake yourself out of the fog that you are living in.

I've found myself in this fog often, where hours, days, or months later, I have no recollection of what was said to me or what happened in those moments. So overwhelmed by grief that you don't think, you don't hear, you don't emote, and you are left wondering if you've remembered to breathe. I've sat with too many folks to count that were in this place. It's a gut-wrenching position to see someone in. Grief so deep that they don't realize what is happening around them. You've been there, haven't you?

A classic scene from the movie, "Saving Private Ryan" gives us a visual for this. As Captain John Miller (Tom Hanks) is on Omaha beach during WWII, there is an explosion that leaves him literally, "shell-shocked". As he loses hearing and tries to bring himself to, he looks up at the chaos that surrounds him. Everything in sight was in complete disarray, but there was nothing he could do. He was helpless, motionless, and unable to think straight. His mind and body were completely overwhelmed and frozen in that moment.

Gary Rydstrom, the sound designer for "Saving Private Ryan," had this to say about that moment in the movie: *"When Tom Hanks is suffering a momentary hearing loss from shell-shock, the visuals don't change much, but we did a radical thing with the sound by shutting down the outside world. You get distorted bits and pieces of the outside, but mostly just this seashell roar as if you're inside his head. There is a wonderful shock coming out of the hearing loss when one of his men is screaming at him to snap to, and now we can hear the guy. There's also a rising tone, like a tea kettle boiling up to that point, then it snaps back to reality. When you are in tense experiences, you have this sense of closing down, almost more aware of your own sounds than the sounds around you. The blood in your ears is going so fast, you're more self-aware than outside aware."* [2]

Sound familiar? Have you felt like you've shut down to the outside world? Stuck in your head while others are trying to get you to "snap to"? Have you closed down or frozen up, becoming deaf to the sounds (people) around you? All the while, you see and feel the chaos and grief that now surrounds you.

If you feel this way, that's OK. It's normal. That's what grief can do. It drops you into this foggy space where you're not completely aware of your surroundings, but so overwhelmed by your grief that you're just left stunned, staring into space, thinking, "how....?"

What "how" questions have you asked or are you currently asking as you grieve?

_____

_____

_____

_____

_____

Why is the word "how" so important here? Why would it be so important that it's the first thing we discuss? The Hebrew word for Lamentations is "Eikah." The word Eikah means, you guessed it, "how". To lament is to outwardly exhibit a sense of sorrow or brokenheartedness. Showing or expressing a sense of misery or being downcast. So, this book of Lamentations is a book of sorrow and grief. It's a book where the pouring out of a broken heart is quite literally asking or crying out, "How?"

To lament goes far deeper than crying or simply letting your emotions out. To lament means to pray. To express that sorrow and grief to God. When we lament, we are laying our pain and sorrow at the feet of Jesus and expressing our trust in Him. You'll see here in a moment that the lament we talk about through this book is a pouring out of the pain and heartache we feel, and yet, choosing to trust Jesus completely in the midst of it all.

Lamentations 3:17-24 is the blueprint for this book. Before we dig into those specific verses, I want you to get a deep understanding of Lamentations and the background behind it. This Old Testament book is a seldomly read, rarely quoted, and an oftentimes misunderstood book of the Bible. In the Introduction to the book of Lamentations in the HCSB Study Bible, it says:

> "This is a book about pain but with hope in God. The author vividly addresses the extremes of human pain and suffering as few other authors have done in history. For this reason, Lamentations is an important biblical source expressing the hard questions that arise during our times of pain." [4]

It is safe to assume that Jeremiah wrote the book of Lamentations. Jeremiah's purpose in writing these poems was in response to the destruction of Jerusalem, the ruin of the temple, and the overall devastation that accompanied it. The Babylonian attack and destruction of Jerusalem was a direct result of the Israelite's rebellion against God, and they knew it. The Israelites experienced much loss, suffering, and agony over the wiping out of their great city. It's out of this extreme grief they are all experiencing what Jeremiah writes. So how does this book of Lamentations help us in our grief? How does it give us any sort of hope?

> *"...how can God's love and justice be reconciled with our pain? Lamentations gives no easy answers to this question, but it helps us meet God in the midst of our suffering and teaches us the language of prayer. Instead of offering a set of techniques, easy answers, or inspiring slogans for facing pain and grief, Lamentations supplies: (1) an orientation, (2) a voice for working through grief from "A to Z," (3) instruction on how and what to pray, and (4) a focal point on the faithfulness of God and the affirmation that He alone is our portion."* [5]
> - **Introduction to the book of Lamentations in the HCSB Study Bible**

In the third chapter of Lamentations, Jeremiah is pouring out all of the grief and hurt and raw emotion of his soul. You can almost feel the affliction and emptiness he is describing. The lack of peace, loss of hope, and even for-getting what happiness is. He goes so far as to say that this suffering is bitter beyond words. Yikes! This is deep, raw, ugly, and painful. You've been there, haven't you? Are you there at this moment? Feeling stuck there?

However, we see Jeremiah do something that we all need to take note of. He does something, that, if we can train our hearts to do likewise, will change our lives forev-er. He changes his thinking. He turns from the bitterness, the hopelessness, and the pain that has overwhelmed his heart. He turns to God. WHILE his heart is hurting, WHILE he grieves, he turns to God. When you read the word "yet", notice the shift in his heart. These are life-changing words for you and I in the midst of our own grief.

> Peace has been stripped away....Everything I had hoped for from the Lord is lost! The thought of my suffering...is bitter beyond words. I will never forget this awful time, as I grieve over my loss. Yet I still dare to hope when I remember this: The faithful love of the Lord never ends! His mercies never cease. Great is his faithfulness; his mercies begin afresh each morning. I say to myself, "The Lord is my inheritance; therefore, I will hope in him!
> - **Lamentations 3:19-24 (NLT)** [6]

We touched ever so slightly on this in the introduction, but did you see it again? I hope you did! I hope it stopped you as soon as the word hit your eyes! "Yet"! I stated this earlier, but I want you to hear it again: "Yet" is a dramatic turn in the posture of our hearts. We start with the reality of the situation that is being faced. Grief has stripped the heart of peace, there is bitter suffering that you cannot seem to shake. YET (although those things are true), there is a greater truth going on here. God is faithful. His love never ends. His mercies never cease, and those mercies are even new for you and I each morning. So, because of these incredible truths, because He is risen, because He is alive and living in and through those we love Him, we can hope in Him!

Note that he didn't have to get healthy and stop grieving in order to turn to God. He simply turned to God and reminded himself of God's goodness right there in the midst of the yuck. I'm confident that as you navigate your grief journey while looking to Jesus, you are going to see this same transformation in your heart.

Which of Jeremiah's words before the "yet" do you most resonate with? Which of Jeremiah's words after the "yet" did you most need to hear right now?

_____

_____

_____

_____

_____

I want you to picture a U-turn sign for a moment. If I'm being completely transparent with you, I'm that guy that makes U-turns on a regular basis when there is a big sign

32

hanging over my car that has the slash through it, telling me I'm not allowed to do that. For all of you police officers and generally law-abiding citizens that loathe people like me, I'm sorry. Think about why we make U-turns. It's because we're going in a direction we don't want to and need to turn around and go back toward our intended destination. You see, Jeremiah is on a journey and his heart is a mess. He realizes this and shifts or turns the focus of his heart to the Lord (his intended destination). "Yet" is nothing more than the U-turn of your heart. Still the same journey of grief, but now moving in the correct direction.

To keep with the driving theme for a moment, if you just continue to go straight in your grief, filled with bitterness and lacking peace, you are only going to remain in that place. The further you go, the more bitter you'll become, the less peace you'll experience, until your grief consumes you. But what if, while on this journey of grief, you decided to turn your focus to Jesus. What if, while grieving, you shifted your focus and pulled a U-turn? What would that look like in your heart today? How would today change if your heart pulled a U-turn and focused on Jesus in the midst of your grief?

If I had a singular hope for how this book might assist you in your grief journey, it would help your thinking turn from:

I have Jesus, but I'm completely overwhelmed by grief.
to
I have grief, but I'm completely overwhelmed by Jesus.

Did you notice that the grief doesn't go away when you say this? It doesn't have to. Jesus doesn't expect it to. He doesn't want you to be done grieving so you can trust Him again. He's simply asking you to trust Him in the midst of the grief you are experiencing. I need to say that again because I think you need to hear that again. Read this slowly, take it in, and chew on it. *Jesus is simply asking you to trust Him in the midst of the grief you are experiencing.*

Take a moment to write out or think through your response to that statement.

_____

_____

_____

_____

_____

If you haven't already, you are going to come across people who expect you to stop grieving, or at least stop grieving the way you have. I'm so sorry. You are allowed to grieve in your time and not how someone else would do it or thinks you should do it. We have this incredibly vulnerable moment that Jesus gives us a front-row seat to in John 11:35, which simply tells us, "Jesus wept".[7]

Now, there are many reasons as to why Jesus wept in this moment, which we won't delve into right now. But the setting in which he wept? His friend, Lazarus, had just passed away. Jesus' response? Weeping. That's next-level crying, which we are all familiar with. Jesus' eyes didn't just well up with tears. I'm confident in saying that He bawled.

He sobbed. He snot-cried. We often don't picture Jesus like this, do we? It's OK to because that's who He is. While fully God, He was fully man and grieved appropriately. So, if Jesus can grieve heavily, if Jesus can snot-cry, so can you.

While we cry, grieve, stare off into space, thinking, "how is this happening to me?", as Christians we can do as Jeremiah did. We can say, "my heart is broken, AND YET, God is loving, God is faithful, God is merciful, and I'm choosing to find my hope in Him."

I want to take you through a short season in our life. My wife, Cathie, and I were about 7 years into marriage. We had recently brought our two boys home from Ethiopia. Coming off a long and grueling season of infertility, it felt like life was normal again. We were having fun and enjoying life for what seemed like the first time in a while. Then, Cathie's mom, Sandi, was diagnosed with cancer, which returned from when she first battled it 12 years prior. Two weeks later, our youngest son, Bowen, was diagnosed with autism. We spent that year watching from across the county as Sandi deteriorated physically. The stress of our son's diagnosis and how to serve him well was just an added tension in our hearts.

Then, it happened. Cathie got the call from her brother, saying, "it's time." I'll let her take it from here...

To say that my mom and I were close would be an understatement. She was my person. The person you give your first call to when struggle or celebration enters your life. It wasn't just me, though. She was a lot of people's person. The difference is that I was lucky to be her person in return.

I remember that brisk September day in 2015 like it was yesterday. We learned that mom had breast cancer for the second time. The words "stage four" were thrown around and I knew this was it. The road may be long but this was the road that would lead to the end. Mom had been cancer free in July and by September of the same year, it had trespassed into every nook and cranny it could find.

Mom chose to fight because that's who she had always been. She was equal parts scrappy and sparkle, so fight she did. Some of her last words to me were, "I want more time." She had more fight in her but the cancer was prevailing.

She fought like a prize fighter. Meanwhile, I was preparing for the end. My hope clung to additional days, not more years. Prior grief in my life had taught me that life-and-death situations don't always end the way that I want them too. And yet, regardless of how the cards fall, I know who is on the throne.

I knew that regardless of how many earthly days my mom had left, she was going to win. Either she would be cancer free on this earth or cancer free in the arms of her Creator. My hope was not a little "h" hope in science, medicine, or radiation. My hope was a big "H" hope, believing that our sovereign God was (and still is) in control and that mom was better in His hands than mine.

In September of 2016, mom, my best friend and my person, was welcomed into the arms of her Creator. I grieved and cried enough tears to fill the Grand Canyon. I missed her. I needed her to tell me everything was going to be okay again. YET, I knew that she was in a far better place than this world *had for her. I knew that she was in a place with no more cancer, no more heartache, and no more fear. While I still lived in the world she left behind, and while this world felt a little darker, I found peace knowing that death hadn't dulled her sparkle. She was at home and she was at peace with Jesus.*

There is not a pretty bow that I can put on this story. I miss her everyday. Yet, I know that she is with her Abba Father and that we will be reunited some day.

As you would imagine and as you might be experiencing yourself, we were distraught. Cathie and I grieved very differently and it often came out at different times. We weren't prepared to grieve, although we knew for a while that this day was coming. However, there is one thing we did together that allowed us to move forward in our grief. We trusted Jesus. It wasn't always easy, to tell you the truth. But, we chose to cling to Jesus in our brokenness and He sustained us. I look back now and see just how faithful He was to us in a dark and difficult season of life. We didn't do anything special and we certainly didn't follow some magic formula for how to grieve well that I'm about to share with you. It was a simple choice that we had to make each day. We trusted Jesus.

Will you allow yourself to grab hold of Jesus in the midst of your pain? I know you are overwhelmed. I know this hurts. I know you have unanswered questions. I know you are battling anger, anxiety, hopelessness, loneliness, insomnia, and so much more. But can we, together, take steps from saying "*I have Jesus, but I'm completely* overwhelmed by grief" to, "I have grief, but I'm completely overwhelmed by Jesus"?

As exhausting as grief can be, and as much of a toll as it takes on our physical and emotional states, there is strength for the believer through Jesus. Remain, not only focused on Him, but in His word, being constantly reminded of His truth. And ask Him to impress His word on your heart when you are just unable to read or focus. Today, maybe this is the simple prayer you need to go to Him with:

> I am weary from grief; strengthen me through your word.
> - **Psalm 119:28 (CSB)** [8]

At this moment, as you endure the weariness of grief, ask the Lord to strengthen you. Take the prayer of Psalm 119:28 and personalize it here:

_____

_____

_____

_____

_____

CHAPTER 2

YOUR GRIEVING HEART

I have to admit to you that I don't grieve well and I especially don't show emotion well. I tend to bottle up my emotions and keep them to myself. Part of that, I believe, is being a man, as we tend to bottle up emotions. Another part of that is being a Quillet (I come from a family that doesn't emote well). Yet, another part of that is my own sinful pride and feeling the need to be strong for everyone around me. And although my wife can always read where my heart is at, and thus, calls me out on it (I love that about her), I do a good job of putting on a mask when I'm hurting.

Looking back on my time as a pastor, I wish I had modeled this better than I did. I put up a good, strong front because so many were looking to me for help in the midst of their own grief. So, I bottled up my emotions. I felt, oftentimes, like I wasn't allowed to grieve in the presence of others because of my role (like, I had to be the strong one). So, I often found myself doing it alone. I can't tell you how often I escaped to our little secluded chapel space, away from the daily goings-on of the church, away from my office where people might see me emotional, and I'd just sit, pray, and cry. The emotion was there. The hurt was there. Those tears, those emotions, that grief...it HAS to be let out. It's OK to grieve and it doesn't have to be done in seclusion. Both knowingly and unknowingly, I've long grieved in seclusion. I'm coming to realize just how poorly I've grieved over the years because I rarely seek support or share what's going on in my heart with anyone. I need to take my words to heart right now that it's OK to grieve.

There is no right or wrong way to grieve. I want to make clear that you and I are allowed to grieve as we need. We have permission. We are allowed to grieve when others are around. We are allowed to grieve instead of trying to be the tough one or the one who has it all together. We are allowed to grieve when it may be awkward for someone else. We do not have to put a mask on with a big smiley face to make everyone think that we are OK. My failures in this have driven me to help you and so many others grieve in a way that not only honors the Lord, but brings your heart to cling fully to Him. Grieving is OK and it is necessary.

Let's not sugarcoat this, alright? Your heart hurts, but it's OK for your heart to hurt and let others know it, as you feel comfortable doing. Don't ever let anyone tell you that it's not. Don't ever let anyone tell you that you should be somewhere else in your grief than where you are. Everyone grieves differently and for different periods of time. Now, this doesn't give you the go-ahead to just do, say or act however you want just because you are grieving. However, let's acknowledge that this is incredibly hard and we're all there at some level.

Where are you in your grief as you read this? Think about this for a moment before continuing on. What are you feeling? What thoughts and emotions tend to dominate your heart and mind? How would you describe the emotional state of your heart right now?

_____

_____

_____

_____

_____

No matter where you are in your grief journey, your heart is aching at a certain level. Surely you have asked God, "why"? Through heavy tears and a broken heart, I'm confident you've either poured out your heart to God at this time or maybe you've tried and just can't get it out. As you read through these various Psalms, allow your heart to speak this outpouring to the Lord as you resonate with what is being spoken.

Psalm 13:1-3 (NLT) - 1 _O Lord, how long will you forget me? Forever? How long will you look the other way? 2 How long must I struggle with anguish in my soul, with sorrow in my heart every day?...3 Turn and answer me, O Lord my God! Restore the sparkle to my eyes, or I will die._ [9]

Psalm 22:1-2 (NLT) - 1 _My God, my God, why have you abandoned me? Why are you so far away when I groan for help? 2 Every day I call to you, my God, but you do not answer. Every night I lift my voice, but I find no relief._ [10]

Psalm 42:3-5 (NLT) - **3** *Day and night I have only tears for food, while my enemies continually taunt me, saying, "Where is this God of yours?"* **4** *My heart is breaking as I remember how it used to be.....* **5** *Why am I discouraged? Why is my heart so sad?* [11]

Psalm 73:13-14 (NLT) - **13** *Did I keep my heart pure for nothing? Did I keep myself innocent for no reason?* **14** *I get nothing but trouble all day long; every morning brings me pain.* [12]

Psalm 10:1 (NLT) - **1** *O Lord, why do you stand so far away? Why do you hide when I am in trouble?* [13]

Psalm 69:1-3 (NLT) - **1** *Save me, O God, for the floodwaters are up to my neck.* **2** *Deeper and deeper I sink into the mire; I can't find a foothold. I am in deep water, and the floods overwhelm me.* **3** *I am exhausted from crying for help; my throat is parched. My eyes are swollen with weeping, waiting for my God to help me.* [14]

Did any of this meet you where you are at currently? Did any of these verses make you say, "THIS IS ME! *This is the cry of my heart right now!*" I hate the brokenness behind these words, as I've felt this before, but I love the model we see throughout the Psalms of pouring out one's heart to the Lord. You have permission to grieve by pouring out to the Lord, asking Him tough questions, and stating just how wounded or bitter your heart has become.

> "Apart from the presence of God, there is no deep healing for our grief. Time can make it easier, but that is all. The good news when our hearts are

broken is that God invites us to freely mourn in the great space of His loving presence. Our pain does not threaten Him; it does not cause Him to fear that we will ruin His reputation. He is not repulsed with the ugliness we feel. Even when we hurt so much that we can hardly bear it, we are still His beloved." [15]
-Sally Breedlove, Choosing Rest

Our God is a personal God. He wants to hear your heart. All of it. He is not far off. He is not stoic. He is not offended by the state of your heart and how you express it. So if you are angry, tell Him you are angry. If you are completely broken, tell Him how that feels. If you just want to scream a cuss word right now, I promise that He has big enough shoulders to handle it and you aren't going to get in trouble. Go ahead and vomit your soul on HIm, by speaking or writing it out in the space provided here...

_____

_____

_____

_____

_____

SOUL VOMIT

My friend and former boss, Matt Boyers (Author, *Consuming Christ*) has spoken often about vomiting our souls on Jesus and I appreciate how he has taught me this practice. I love the analogy, and everyone seems to understand it well, but it seems that every time I talk about it, I get weird looks. I know this is a disgusting example to use, but it fits too well here not to talk about it. Think for a moment about WHY people vomit. I told you! Don't act surprised by this, I warned you that a gross example was coming. Stick with me though! Why do people vomit? There's something in the stomach that isn't right or might be causing pain, and it needs to come out. And what happens once you've physically vomited? Typically, you feel better! Now, before you continue to read, I apologize for the mental picture I'm about to give you. When I physically vomit, I scream. Not intentionally, I promise. My wife gives me such a hard time for this. I don't know what it is, but when I vomit (which thankfully hasn't been all that much over the years), a LOUD scream comes with it. I don't know the science behind it, but I guess it's as simple as my vocal cords being triggered as I puke. I try my hardest EVERY time not to scream, to no avail. It has become a pretty comical thing in our home when it does happen, so I typically don't get much compassion when I'm sick because my wife is laughing hysterically at the blood curdling "screams."

Why in the world do I share this with you? I want you to feel the freedom to scream as you vomit your soul on the Lord. Release the pent up emotion. Let it out. Don't hold back. What has been festering in your spirit that you need to just scream at Him? What emotions or questions or confusion has been bubbling below the surface that needs to explode? You have the freedom to protest your circumstances. You have the freedom to outwardly process your emotions to Him. Go ahead and voice your confusion. Ask Him the difficult questions that you need an answer to.

In Mark 4, we find Jesus and the disciples out on a boat. While many of these former fishermen are in their element on the sea, something happens that brings them to their knees. A storm pops up and the waves are crashing over the boat. Although they would have felt incredibly comfortable out on the open water, I'm sure they knew too many people who had been taken by the sea over the years. So, they were understandably scared as they watched their rickety boat get beat on by these waves. Where was Jesus? Oh, He was in the stern of the boat...sleeping! And how do the disciples respond to Jesus? By pouring out the emotion of their hearts. "DON'T YOU CARE THAT WE'RE GOING TO DIE!?!?"

Now, Jesus got right up, calmed the storm, and all was OK in their world again. But let's think about this for a moment. Are you in that place currently? The place that says, "Jesus, don't you care?"

- *Don't you care how broken I am?*
- *Don't you care how sad I am?*

- Don't you care how much my heart hurts?
- Don't you care that I'm anxious and overwhelmed right now?
- Don't you care how lonely I am?
- Don't you care that this is affecting my marriage and relationships?
- Don't you care that I'm running out of tears?
- Don't you care that this is drawing me away from You?
- Don't you care that I just lost another person that I love?
- Don't you care about ME?

Jesus, DON'T YOU CARE!?!? Are you sleeping? Where are you?

Ever been there? I have. It's OK to have been there. It's OK if you're there right now. It's OK if you are asking Him really difficult questions. It's OK to ask why and to wonder where He is or if He even cares. It's OK to let Him know you aren't at peace. It's OK to tell Him how hopeless you feel, how bitter you've become, and how awful this all is. It's even OK to tell Him that it feels like He's distant or not listening.

We see Jeremiah do exactly this in Lamentations 3:17-20.

> **Peace has been stripped away....Everything I had hoped for from the Lord is lost! The thought of my suffering...is bitter beyond words. I will never forget this awful time, as I grieve over my loss.** [16]

These gut-wrenching words make it clear that any sense of peace that he once felt has vanished. In his mind, he feels that he's lost everything. He's suffering. He's bitter. And he'll never forget this awful season and the loss he's endured. Sound familiar? Like Jeremiah, you aren't going to forget this awful time. You aren't just going to forget about the person you love so much that you've lost.

In the introduction, I shared with you some of the most extreme grief experiences I've had. The losses of those who were dear to me and I felt the pain of their loss in an extremely heavy way. I ended each story with, "I'll never forget this awful time". It's true. You don't ever forget that awful time. It sticks with you. It becomes part of you. It's ingrained in your heart and mind for the rest of your life. It changes you. You don't just one day, all of a sudden, move along from it. You'll never forget the person you loved so much that is no longer here with you. Ever.

There is a heartbreak that my wife, Cathie, and I carry every day. We're members of a grieving fraternity that never had the pleasure of meeting those we grieve so hard for. You see, over the course of many years, we experienced four miscarriages. We never got to meet our four children, who once had strong heartbeats. Trust me, I heard those beating hearts, and they were some of the most beautiful sounds my ears have ever heard. Infertility and miscarriage grief is a different animal all in itself. If you've experienced the loss of an unborn child, you know that many people do not acknowledge it as "real" grief. The well-meaning but absolutely cruel and heartbreaking comments from ignorant people are difficult to endure. We've been there, and if miscarriage is a part of your story, I am so sorry. I will say, if you are a member of this fraternity, or know someone who is, check out The Quillet Institute online. My wife, Cathie, has some incredible resources specifically for you!

Throughout the years that we lost our four babies, I often cried out to God, "Don't you care?" It certainly felt like He was asleep as we endured loss after loss. Those were hard times of grief, but also hard times of trusting God as we had to say goodbye to each of our children that we had so many hopes and dreams for, and more than anything, just couldn't wait to hold in our arms. It never happened. We were confused, broken, feeling alone, and really questioning what God was doing.

So not only is there the grief that comes from the loss of our loved ones but even as Christians, there is this sense of, "Really, God?" There are so many promises throughout scripture, many that we discuss in this book. Promises like: He hears us, He's faithful to us, He's present with us, He answers our prayers, etc.

We read in Zephaniah 3:17 (CSB)

> The Lord your God is among you, a warrior who saves. He will rejoice over you with gladness. He will be quiet in his love. He will delight in you with singing. [17]

We hear God say in Isaiah 41:10 (CSB):

> Do not fear, for I am with you; do not be afraid, for I am your God. I will strengthen you; I will

*help you; I will hold on to you with my righteous
right hand.* [18]

We read these promises and it leaves us thinking, "but
what about me? Is this not true for me?" And so, we don't
like to admit this out loud, but we have these thoughts that
maybe God has let us down. That He didn't follow through.
That He wasn't faithful. That He didn't hear my prayers. That
He failed to hold up His end of the deal. Right? I've certainly been there. As Christians, we think these things, but we
rarely share these thoughts with others, or even with Him.
But, that lack of peace, that loss of hope, that bitterness, it's
all taking up residence in our hearts.

Now, it's OK to question God and wonder why or how
this is all happening. It's good to wrestle with God in these
moments.

Dr. Lois Evans, the wife of Dr. Tony Evans, passed away
on December 30th, 2019. This is a family that I look to with
much respect because of their great love for Jesus and how
they've used their platforms to point people to Him. At Lois'
funeral, their son, Jonathan, gave the eulogy. Here is a snip-
pet of what he said:

> *I was wrestling with God because I said, well—if
> we have victory in Your name, didn't You hear us
> when we were praying?*
> *Didn't you hear all of those prayers? Didn't You
> hear us? Where are You? Why didn't You do what
> we were asking of You, because Your Word says,*

*that if we abide in You and in—Your Word abides
in us and we can ask whatever we will and it will
be given to us. Your Word tells us that if we ask
according to Your will, that You hear us.
Your Word is, is telling us that—in Mark 11, If you
pray believing, you will receive. To be anxious
for nothing but through prayer and supplication,
make your requests known. Where are You? I was
wrestling with God the last few days because this
was a great opportunity that we can tangibly see
Your glory. Everybody was praying—not only in
Dallas but around the country and around the
world; people were watching. Where are You?
This was an opportunity for us to see Your glory.* [19]

Jonathan went on to say that God responded and spoke
some hard truths to him. Sometimes we need to hear those
hard truths. Job needed to hear those hard truths after
questioning God. See, questioning God is ok, but we have
to know that He is going to respond with truth. We don't
always like to hear that truth in the moment, but it's necessary. You and I need to be reminded that our minds can't
think like God's. He says so Himself in Isaiah 55:8.

*"For my thoughts are not your thoughts, and your
ways are not my ways." This is the Lord's decla-
ration.* [20]

We cannot understand His ways. We cannot think as He

thinks. We cannot comprehend why He would allow what He allows. However, we can trust Him, even when it doesn't make sense.

My encouragement to you is, that while trusting Him, keep asking hard questions. Continue to pour out your emotions to Him. Let Him hear the state of your heart often. And, as you do this, He will be faithful to respond. As He responds, I think you're going to find a next level of peace that you didn't have before. Over time, the more you trust Him and the more He shows His faithfulness to you, the more healing you're going to see. This healing is an ongoing process, and by ongoing, I mean it will probably be a life-long process.

I don't say this to be "Debbie Downer," but the unfortunate reality is this grief in your heart will always be with you on this earth. Always. That's not pessimism speaking. That's not hopelessness speaking. That's the truth.

Your heart is always going to experience a level of hurt as you grieve the loss of your loved one(s). Now, that grief and heartache looks different over the course of weeks, months, and years. My guess is that if you have been grieving the loss of a loved one for many years, your grief looks different today than it did on day one. Some good and healthy language that was shared with me years ago is that "you never move on, but you CAN move forward." We can move forward into relationships, into work, into church involvement, into our day-to-day. Moving forward doesn't mean you are ignoring and moving away from your grief. Moving forward doesn't mean you stop thinking about or you forget your loved one. Moving forward isn't a heartless or uncompassionate step. It is healthy to move forward and we have good reason to do so on this journey. This act of moving forward is nothing more than the healing that is taking place in your heart. It probably feels slow-going sometimes, but continue to trust in Him as He heals your broken heart.

This whole "moving forward" thing might sound ridiculous to you. Maybe you aren't ready for that just yet. Maybe you just don't want to. Maybe you just feel stuck. So let's "move forward" into Jeremiah's pouring out. He shares the state of his soul. It's ugly. It's broken. It's messy and angry and full of questions and seriously lacking peace. Then, he's reminded of the truth he has long known. He recalls good news that he has clung to in the past. In this moment, something happens in his heart.

"Yet"...

CHAPTER 3

CHOOSING TO LIVE IN THE "YET"

It was the fall of my senior year of high school. Late one night, some friends and I decided to go to the movie theatre in a nearby city. On the way home from the movie, the guy driving ended up in a cornfield and flipped his SUV 4 times. It was past midnight and we were out in the middle of nowhere, also known as the sprawling cornfield hell of northwest Ohio. No cell phones, no nearby homes, nothing.

I actually have some vivid memories of the moments after I woke up. I looked around and saw chaos. Actually, it felt like that scene from "Saving Private Ryan" we read about earlier. Smoke coming from the car, a shattered but intact windshield, and some badly injured friends. I was so confused by what all had just happened. I was completely overwhelmed at the moment and I didn't know what to do. After some time, I crawled out the back passenger side door, and it all kind of hit me. I looked myself over and figured that I was OK enough to go get help. I then remembered where we were and what road we were on when the accident happened. I knew of a house down the road. As moments went by, I remembered more and more of what was going on and what I needed to do. I had a clear enough picture of my situation to move forward, and that's just what I did. I walked to the house down the road, knocked until they woke up, and asked them to call 911. In the midst of chaos, I had some clarity.

In the midst of Jeremiah's own personal anguish, there was a moment of clarity. At that moment, he remembered God's faithfulness and He spoke that truth in trust.

Just as I felt confused and overwhelmed by the moment in my accident, Jeremiah was overwhelmed and confused as he poured out his broken heart. We read earlier of his lack of peace, his internal suffering, his newfound bitterness, and the fact that he'd never forget this awful time. At that moment, Jeremiah had a choice. It's the same choice you and I are facing. Do we remain in hopelessness? Do we live out each day lacking peace? Do we just sit in our grief, reminding ourselves of what happened, and how miserable we are? Do we continue to wall ourselves off from those relationships we once held so dear? Do we dwell in anger, bitterness, frustration, loneliness, and pain? Do we sit and stew and allow this to eat us up from the inside, or do we make a choice to shift the focus of our hearts while we grieve?

"Yet"

Jeremiah goes on to say in Lamentations 3, "**Yet I still dare to hope when I remember this: The faithful love of the Lord never ends! His mercies never cease. Great is his faithfulness; his mercies begin afresh each morning. I say to** myself, *"The Lord is my inheritance; therefore, I will hope in him!"* [21]

In the midst of his grief, he remembers God's love! He remembers God's mercy! He remembers God's faithfulness! He remembers that his hope is found in God and God alone! And, so, what does Jeremiah choose to do? He makes this statement: "Therefore, I will hope in Him."

We'll dig deeper into the hope we have in Jesus in the next chapter. You and I can never move forward in our grief without hope. There's nothing to live for without hope in Jesus. There's no chance of healing or redemption without hope. Jesus is the ONLY hope we'll ever find, and so choosing to cling to our hope in Him is all we've got. Hope is found in the death and resurrection of Jesus and we cling to the truth that He will complete what He has begun. At a certain point, we HAVE to begin reminding ourselves of the truth of God that we know. We have to not only be reminded of it, but we've got to also live it.

The healthiest grievers I've ever met are those who constantly remain focused on Jesus in the midst of their grief. They remind themselves of Jesus often, remain in His word, and don't allow their hearts to stray. They trust the Holy Spirit to give them what they need day by day. The most unhealthy grievers I've ever met are those who stray from the truths they once knew well. They've not remained students of scripture. They've turned from God. They've turned to lifestyles that are not God-honoring. They've allowed their hearts to stray and they've become bitter, hopeless, and lacking peace. They tried to find satisfaction in things other than Christ. I believe, simply because they did not remain in Jesus as He called us to do in John 15. They failed to remind themselves of Him, stay connected to Him, and allow Him to nourish them. Instead, they became all-consumed by the grief. For those people, it has not gone well.

For those who have remained in Jesus, continuing to glean from His word and constantly reminding themselves of who He is, even in their grief, there has been a constant joy, even in the heartache. There's been peace, even in the hurt. There's been hope, even in the gut-wrenching pain. Because of Jesus.

In Lamentations 3, Jeremiah begins speaking to himself. He begins reminding himself of the truth that he already knows. He begins teaching his heart all over again that this truth is what I'm going to cling to.

It's like he goes from, "Everything is awful, I have no peace, and I'm angry....but wait a second, I know God loves me and he's merciful towards me and He's faithful to me. He always has been. So, if this is true of God (and it is), then I'm going to choose to find my hope in Him!" He speaks this to himself!

There are moments when you are feeling at your absolute worst. Your lowest. Where you are experiencing the most pain and heartache. When you've lost the peace you once had and are feeling hopeless. When the grief seems to be overwhelming you the most. It's in those moments that you have to preach the truth of God to yourself. You cannot wait for a pastor to tell you the truth of scripture, you have to do this for yourself. Tell yourself the truth of the gospel. Tell yourself how much God loves you. Tell yourself of the hope you have in Jesus because of what He has done and what He is doing. Preach of His faithfulness and mercy toward you. Preach the word to yourself and allow your heart to receive it. You may not be a "preacher," but if you are a Christian, you know God's word. You know the truth. So you give your heart the most fiery, passionate sermon you can imagine based on God's incredible love for you and presence with you. Your heart needs this and it needs it often!

Years ago, I was encouraged to pray often for the moments in my future that would be difficult. To ask God to remind me of Himself when I was overwhelmed by circumstances. This was revolutionary for me. It's an incredibly important prayer because I don't trust myself to immediately think of Him when I get overwhelmed. I can oftentimes get so caught up in the mess that it's almost like I forget He's with me. So, if I'm prone to forget about Him when I'm grieved or stressed or hurting, I need to pray in the now, when my head is clear, that He would remind me of Himself in those moments. Maybe this prayer could look something like this for you:

> Jesus, I acknowledge that when my heart is overwhelmed, I focus on my circumstances instead of you. Please forgive me for my lack of trust in those moments. Because my heart and mind seem to have blinders on in those difficult times, will you please remind me of You. As I focus on

the pain, would you gently whisper to me your
love, your care, and your heart for me? Would my
heart become quickly reminded of you so that I
may turn to you, think about you, dwell in Your
word, and trust you in ways I hadn't been before?
Jesus, help me with my unbelief, my lack of trust,
and my focus on those things that are not from
you. Help me to remember and trust you. Thank
you, Jesus. Amen

Friend, as you pray this prayer, God is faithful to not only hear you but act upon this for you. I'd encourage you to pray this so that as He reminds you of Himself, you can begin to think of Him and speak those truths you know of Him immediately as you walk through difficulty.

If you, as broken as you may feel, are going to take steps to move forward, you must begin speaking to yourself. Speaking with confidence to who you are and the truth you know about the God who is present with you, loves you, and is at work for you! Martyn Lloyd-Jones says this perfectly, so I'll just stop talking and let his words speak to you...

The main trouble in this whole matter of spiritu-
al depression in a sense is this, that we allow our
self to talk to us instead of talking to our self....
Have you realized that most of your unhappiness
in life is due to the fact that you are listening to
yourself instead of talking to yourself? Take those
thoughts that come to you the moment you wake

up in the morning. You have not originated them, but they start talking to you, they bring back the problem of yesterday, etc. Somebody is talking. Who is talking to you? Your self is talking to you.... The main art in the matter of spiritual living is to know how to handle yourself. You have to take yourself in hand, you have to address yourself, preach to yourself, question yourself. You must say to your soul: 'Why art thou cast down'–what business have you to be disquieted? You must turn on yourself, upbraid yourself, condemn yourself, exhort yourself, and say to yourself: 'Hope thou in God'–instead of muttering in this depressed, un-happy way. And then you must go on to remind yourself of God, Who God is, and what God is and what God has done, and what God has pledged Himself to do. Then having done that, end on this great note: defy yourself, and defy other people, and defy the devil and the whole world, and say with this man: 'I shall yet praise Him for the help of His countenance, who is also the health of my countenance and my God'. [22]

–D. Martyn Lloyd-Jones, *Spiritual Depression: Its Causes and Cure*

What truth of God do you need to speak to yourself in this moment? What one thing does your heart need to be reminded of right now? Don't just write it out, but also speak it to yourself.

_____

_____

_____

_____

_____

When you begin speaking truth to yourself about who God is, what He has done, what His promises are, and how you've experienced his faithfulness in the past, then you WILL begin taking steps toward healing. It is this truth of God that brings joy. It is this truth of God that brings hope. Hope to move forward and hope to press on. Hope to live the life that God has given you. We have hope because of what He has done, and nothing, not even the loss of your dearest loved one, can take away the hope we have in Christ Jesus.

So, even though we live with broken hearts, we can still hope because of what Christ has done, is doing, and will do. And this is why we can confidently say, "yet." We can move forward saying things like, *"This is hard,* **yet**, *He is faithful and as someone who trusts in Christ, I know what is ahead for me, both here on this earth and when I'm with Him in Glory!*

I love the "yet" language that is used throughout scripture. Jeremiah uses it here in Lamentations and we see David use it masterfully throughout the Psalms. It's this pouring out of the heart that says, *"God, here is my reality.*

Here's what I'm facing. Here's what I'm up against. Here's the state of my hurting heart. It's hard. I'm not doing well. **Yet** *(or oftentimes the word, "but" is used), here's what I know to be true."* It's a reminder to your own heart that although your reality and experiences are one thing, your heart knows something greater is going on here and the truth of God's word says that there is hope.

It doesn't come easy or naturally in grief to just reply with a "yet". Especially when our hearts are in a position of saying, *"I'll never forget this awful time as I grieve over my loss"*. That in itself just feels hopeless, doesn't it? And so, it takes a lot for our hearts to turn from hopelessness to hope. Our hearts and minds have to be trained. Trained with God's truth written on our hearts and in our minds. As Jeremiah said, *"Yet I still dare to hope when I remember this"*. He KNEW God's truth, and so, in the midst of his grief, he called it to mind. He remembered it and it brought him to the place of responding with, "yet". We'll focus much more on this in the coming pages, but I want our hearts to begin to resonate with Jeremiah's words of heartbreak while looking ahead to the incredible hope that is present and available!

In the grief you are experiencing, you continue to feel a mixed bag of emotions, don't you? Maybe even a new or different one as each day begins. Hopelessness, anger, confusion, denial, depression, loneliness, jealousy, shock, bitterness, apathy, disorganization, resentment, brokenness, guilt, helplessness, fear, denial....and the list goes on. I obviously haven't covered them all, but I'm sure you resonate with at least a few of these. Maybe even right now at this moment you feel consumed by one or more of them. So what do we do? How do we find hope in the midst of this? How do we begin to move forward with sad and hurting hearts?

His name is Jesus. He is the ONLY source of hope we could ever have. And as you read on, you're going to see promise after promise from our God, granting our hearts real hope in the midst of our hurt, our pain, our broken-ness, and for many of us, our feelings of hopelessness.

Now claim the truths that you know about Jesus. State why your heart is secure and safe under the shadow of His wings. Write out your version of what Jeremiah wrote in Lamentations 3:21-24 as he declares who God is and why His heart will be OK....

_____

_____

_____

_____

_____

FOCUS SHIFTED

Jess and Rachel are dear friends of ours. Jess is also our pastor and he has taught me much about how to grieve in the "yet". Truly, there are few people whom I know who model living in the "yet" like Jess and Rachel. I want you to hear their story, and I want you to see how messy Jess' grief was. More importantly, I want you to see that even someone who models the "yet" well still struggles in the midst of their grief. I appreciate Jess' honesty and transparency here as he shares their story of grief and how God has re-focused Jess' heart in the midst of grief.

We make the drive every year on his birthday.

That day also happens to be the day he died.

The drive is about an hour long. There's a peacefulness about it, especially when we get off the interstate and onto the country backroads. But there's also a somberness about the drive. Each turn we take seems to bring back a new memory.

The first time we made that drive, I never fathomed I would be driving to a family member's grave as a 27-year-old father, especially my son's grave. I don't think it will ever seem natural; parents are not supposed to bury their children.

My son's death came suddenly. My wife, Rachel, and I were celebrating so much in life. We were celebrating a new position in ministry that God had called us to. We were excited as I was ending my seminary education. God had blessed us with an energetic fifteen-month-old named Canon. And our second son, Will, would soon be born.

We moved to Tennessee to join a new ministry in January 2011. On February 6, 2011, Rachel and I found ourselves in the hospital dealing with the news that our son, Will, was going to be delivered and would not live very long after birth.

I remember the words the doctor told me like it was yesterday. Our son, outside of the womb, would be "incompatible with life."

Our world came crashing down.

We were not prepared for the death of our son. About the only thing we could do was cry. In the months following Will's death, we began to cope with our loss. We began to find our new normal as parents who lost a child.

What I wasn't prepared for is what the months and years of grief would do. I wasn't prepared for the lies I would believe about grief.

The first lie that I bought into was that I had to be strong. That first year, I hid my grief in my work. I told myself that I had to be the strong one. I told myself that if I didn't keep it together, then everything would come crashing down. So anytime I felt grief, I worked. I worked the pain away. The more grief I felt, the harder I worked. I worked 10 hours a day, 7 days a week. I was strong on the outside, but a wreck on the inside.

Grief told me another lie. I believed the lie that my wife should grieve the same way I was grieving. I didn't understand her new routine and habits. I didn't understand her random-to-me tears. I didn't know why watching a particular tv show meant so much to her. And I didn't seek to understand. I just watched from the outside, looking in, and wondering.

I believed the lie that grief has the same timetable for everyone. As the months and years passed, I believed that I needed to move on. I believed that since people stopped asking about my son that I shouldn't be thinking about my son. And clearly, the tears were less, so my grief should be less. I was wrong.

And then there was the lie that my marriage would heal my grief. I believed that my wife would be the one to help me get through my pains and struggles. Not only did she not know what I was feeling because I hid it in my work, but I expected her to figure out my grief as well. My expectations grew and so did my distance from her.

CHOOSING TO LIVE IN THE "YET"

Our marriage was sent into a death spiral. We were lost. We didn't know which way was up and which way was down. The pit was dark and deep. We couldn't see the light.

But, Jesus intervened.

But, God showed up.

But, the Holy Spirit began working in unexpected ways.

Truth began to slowly move from the mind into my heart. I began to look at my work, my wife, and my grief differently. I began to see God's plan for my life in ways I hadn't before.

What changed?

My grief didn't disappear. In fact, my grief grew. It had been piled up for far too long and it was time to deal with it.

So what changed? The purpose of my grief changed.

My wife and I had the chance to meet with another couple who were knowingly about to experience a loss of their own. We were about to talk with them, cry with them, and just be there for them.

And just like that, my grief had a purpose. My wounds began to heal. The lies I believed were shattered. The truth won.

When we seek God's purpose for our grief, God begins to use our grief in ways we never thought possible. When God puts purpose to grief, it's powerful.

While I wish I never would have walked the path I did, I am thankful the journey has taken me to where I am today. My wounds turned into scars. My scars show the power of God's healing.

Don't rid yourself of grief, find the purpose in your grief. And watch God move.

We'll keep making the drive to my son's grave every year, multiple times a year. I'll continue crying. I'll continue grieving. My tears will be strong tears of grief. I still long to simply give my son a hug. But the tears will also be tears of joy. I cannot wait until I have that sweet reunion with my little boy in heaven. It will be such a tremendous joy, a joy that only comes from the Lord.

Friends, I hope you saw in Jess' story that moving from, "hopelessness", to "yet", to "hope-filled trust" doesn't happen overnight. My desire is that this book would help encourage you to take steps forward. I want to give you a short but powerful scripture that I'd encourage you to memorize and speak out to the Lord daily.

We do not know what to do, but our eyes are on you.
- 2 Chronicles 20:12, The MSG Translation [23]

I love this! Basically, it's, "I have no other options and I don't know how to move forward, so I'm going to focus solely on you, God." This is God's desire for us. That we would go nowhere but to Him. That we'd focus on He and He alone because there is nowhere else to turn that can satisfy. He is all we have, and this scripture is a crying out of trust. Go ahead and speak these things to HIm if they pertain to you:

- "Jesus, I don't know HOW to move forward. I don't know what steps to take. I don't know what to do today. I don't

know how to function at this moment. I don't know what to do. But, I'm choosing to fix my eyes on you."
- "I'm stressed. It hurts. I am overwhelmed. I am tired. I am beaten down. I don't know what to do anymore. BUT, My eyes are fixed on you."
- "Jesus, this is miserable and I hate it. BUT, I trust you. I am focusing on you. I am going to let you lead me. I am clinging to you. You are all I have."
- "Jesus, I miss _____ . I do not understand why you allowed them to be taken from this earth. I am angry / sad / hurt / confused / lonely / broken. I don't know how to live without them, but I'm going to choose to fix my eyes on you.
- "I have turned away from you and clung to other things. I've lost my peace, my hope, and my love for you. I've doubted you. I've not trusted you. I have taken my eyes off of you. Forgive me. I don't know what to do anymore, but from this moment on, my eyes are fixed on you."

Spend some time writing this out in your own words:

_____

_____

_____

_____

_____

What a beautiful place to be. Hard, for sure, but beautiful. Speak this to Him daily. Tell him how broken you are and you don't know how to move forward, but then also tell Him that you are choosing to trust Him. Keep telling your heart that you're going to choose to trust Him. This is the only way to live out a life of trusting Jesus in the midst of pain.

As a pastor, there were two times I feel like this was my heart's response, as much or more so than at any other time in my life. These are times when I was so broken and overwhelmed that I didn't know what to do as a pastor or leader. My heart was a wreck and I didn't know what to do in the midst of the shock and grief I was experiencing. Early on, I mentioned the stories of Michael and LJ. I'll begin with Michael.

Michael was a quiet, but fun kid. He had been attending our youth group for a year or so. Always with a Mountain Dew in hand and wanting to play video games. One morning before school, Michael and another boy in our youth group walked to a friend's house on their way to school. They waited in the living room as that kid got ready so they could all walk to school together. As Michael and the other boy in our youth group waited, they saw a shotgun laying in the living room. Their friend's dad had already left for work that morning, and, for some reason that I'll never understand, left the gun laying out. Little did these naive junior high boys know, this shotgun was loaded.

The other boy in our youth group picked up the gun and began to mess around by pointing it at Michael. Stupid? Absolutely. But it was not malicious. If he could go back in time, I know he would have never taken this moment so lightly. He told me as much in my multiple visits with him in jail. As he pointed the gun at Michael's chest from a few feet away "in fun", it went off.

I recall the moment I found out like it happened today. I was unlocking the front doors of the church early that Wednesday morning, preparing for our weekly staff meeting when I got the call from Michael's aunt and uncle who attended our church. I ran out to my car and sped to the hospital where I was met by the family, hysterical over the just-announced death of their teenage son.

Jesus, I don't know what to do, but my eyes are fixed on you.

LJ was one of my favorites. Probably not a kid in all my years in youth ministry that I spent more time with. His life was tough and He longed to be discipled, so I did whatever I could to help him and point him to Jesus. LJ had spent his last few years with his aunt and uncle because mom and dad were unable, unwilling, whatever. LJ carried this hurt, this abandonment, this pain with him every day. This kid SO BADLY desired to follow Jesus. We met just about every Friday morning for coffee before school to dig through God's word. He came to our house to hang out and work on projects with me. He was a leader in our youth group. He wanted to be a pastor when he grew up. LJ loved Jesus, but he continued to carry serious baggage from his family and his past. One summer, LJ worked at our church conference's summer camp for a few weeks. I happened to speak at the camp for a week while LJ was there and we spent a lot of time together. I took him and some of his buddies out to dinner for his birthday one night. We spent a lot of time talking. LJ was in a rough place emotionally at that time, so I was glad I got to encourage him that week. My last day there, as I prepared a talk for that evening, I watched him from my air-conditioned room while he shoveled dirt in 100-degree weather. I'd poke my head out from time to time to laugh at him and taunt him from my cool and comfortable room. That's the last time I ever saw LJ.

A few weeks later, back in our hometown, LJ had come home from camp and moved in with another family. I was confident and hopeful this would be a turning point for him. One that would bring him "back". Unfortunately, his past, his family, his self-condemnation, and his deep emotional wounds became too much. LJ, in a state of being completely overwhelmed, went out to the barn where he hung himself. Although he lived a few more days, he was braindead and taken off life support. It was one of the most difficult times of my life.

Jesus, I don't know what to do, but my eyes are fixed on you.

There is always this moment in time where we have to make a choice in our grief. We've seen Jeremiah do this. We've seen David do this. And now, you, if you have not already, HAVE to do this. It's where you draw a line in the sand. It's where you put a stake in the ground. It's where you pour your broken heart out to Jesus, telling him the state of your soul....and then....

YET....

Jesus, I trust you. My eyes are fixed on you. I know you are faithful. You are my source of hope, joy, and peace. So, no matter what my heart is up against, no matter how much pain I feel, I know you are good. I know you are faithful. I know what your word says. I know what my future holds. I KNOW the truth. Therefore, I am choosing to cling to my God who is faithful.

Choosing to live in the "Yet" doesn't mean you stop grieving.

Choosing to live in the "Yet" doesn't mean everything is suddenly going to be fine.

Choosing to live in the "Yet" doesn't mean you move on and forget about your loved one(s).

Choosing to live in the "Yet" doesn't mean you won't fall back into despair from time to time.

Choosing to live in the "Yet" doesn't change any of your circumstances.

Choosing to live in the "Yet" is about more than that. Living in the "Yet" means a turning of our heart and a turning of our mind to Jesus. It's repentance. Repentance is simply a turning back to Jesus. It's a change of thinking from your own sin, emotion, or general lack of focus on Jesus and instead turning back to Him, thinking on Him, looking to Him, and trusting in Him.

Choosing to live in the "Yet" is simply a change in the posture of your heart. It's moving from a focus on your loss and the grief that has ensued and instead placing your focus on Jesus WHILE you grieve your loss. It's remembering who God is in the midst of this terribly difficult time and choosing to trust Him. As you trust Him, and as you seek the Spirit to work in your heart, He is going to give your heart peace. He's going to give your heart joy. He's going to give your heart hope. He's in the business of redemption and healing and although your healing process isn't likely to happen overnight, He will heal the hearts of those who love Him. You can't be a Christ-follower and NOT have joy. It comes with the territory because the Holy Spirit gives it to you. Same with peace. You've experienced His peace in the past when your heart was at a place of unrest. You've been given joy before even though your circumstances were difficult. He'll do this again as you trust Him.

CHOOSING JESUS IN EXTREME HEARTACHE

Renee is a dear friend going back to our college days. She and her husband John were expecting their second child. Due to an unknown infection, Renee went into preterm labor, which could not be stopped. Renee gave birth that day to baby Ella at 21 weeks and 6 days. Ella was on this earth for 44 minutes before her undeveloped lungs could no longer function. John and Renee lost their daughter on what SHOULD have been an incredibly joyous day of celebrating new life. They were obviously devastated.

Renee would be the first to tell you how difficult this journey of grief has been. The waves of emotion have been overwhelming at times. Renee has been a model to me in living in the "yet." This has shaken her faith at times, but through the lack of peace and the bitterness she has felt, just like Jeremiah wrote, she has kept her eyes on Jesus. I asked Renee a question and I want to share her answer with you. I think you'll find yourself nodding your head in agreement, but also encouraged by her faith in the midst of her grief.

I asked Renee what she would say to the person who is overwhelmed by grief, lacking peace, and struggling to find hope in the midst of this season. Her response:

I would say, I get you. I get it. I've struggled too and still do. I still wonder. I still question. I still get angry and upset and cry. I still get anxious and think about our family's future. We want more children. Will we have that? I question a lot of things. But I know, even in the questioning and tears and anger and jealousy, He hears me. He knows. He knows even before I say it. He knows even before I think it. But He still wants me to come to Him because he will help me and knows what is best for me, even if I don't agree at the time. He wants me to pour it all on Him because He can take it. Every bit of it.

You see, we can remain in grief while keeping our eyes focused on Jesus. It's not a choice of Jesus or grief. You don't have to stop grieving in order to cling to and trust Jesus. He's simply asking you to turn your heart to Him AS you grieve. We can turn to and place our focus and trust on Jesus as we continue to mourn our loss. We don't know what to do, so we'll fix our eyes on You. Sing it if you know it, and let this be a worshipful moment, telling your heart what to do and the truth of God that you know, in the midst of your grief...

Turn your eyes upon Jesus,
Look full in His wonderful face,
And the things of earth will grow strangely dim,
In the light of His glory and grace. [24]

CHAPTER 4

CLINGING TO HOPE

After many good years living in Ohio, Cathie and I felt the strong nudge to go. Nashville, Tennessee burned a hole in our hearts, much like Ethiopia did years earlier when we prayed through what part of the world we would pursue adoption. While we were praying through our adoption process back in 2011, we just couldn't shake the thought of Ethiopia. God laid this country and these people so heavily on our hearts. He did the same with Nashville, in a way that is hard to explain other than it was simply the Holy Spirit's leading. We just couldn't shake it.

We visited the Nashville area for the first time ever, and we were not only smitten, but we knew this was where God wanted us to be (despite so many people telling us how crazy and stupid we were). Soon after our move, we visited a church for the first time (it's now our church home and we LOVE our church family). I stood for worship that morning completely overwhelmed. I was in a new town, worshipping in a new church that I wasn't a pastor in (I hadn't done that in 15 years), I had no relationships here, and I still didn't have a job to provide for my family. That week, I had started feeling the nudge to bring this book to fruition and I stood there in worship, overwhelmed by the thought of the book and the recent craziness of our lives. The premise of this book was heavy on me in that moment as I sat in this new church. While stewing in it all, a new song started that I was unaware of. So, I just listened and took it in. The song was, "Do It Again" by Elevation Worship.

I'm hearing and then beginning to sing this song for the first time ever, and then it hit me, "*This is it!*" God's faithfulness to you and I in the midst of difficulty, grief, confusion, pain, _____ (fill in your emotion). His faithfulness to those who trust Him when life is hard and your heart hurts. His promises are ALWAYS true, He is ALWAYS present, and He is ALWAYS enough! In the moment that the Holy Spirit seemed to be laying this book idea on my heart, this song comes along and basically sums up the book. I love how God works!

Maybe you've heard this song, maybe you haven't. If you haven't, grab your phone, get on your computer, tell Alexa or Siri or whatever robot you have to play it, just do whatever you have to do! If you don't have access to listen to it at this moment, just read these words and take them in.

> *Walking around these walls*
> *I thought by now they'd fall*
> *But You have never failed me yet*
> *Waiting for change to come*

Knowing the battle's won
For You have never failed me yet

[Chorus]

Your promise still stands
Great is Your faithfulness, faithfulness
I'm still in Your hands
This is my confidence, You've never failed me yet

I know the night won't last
Your Word will come to pass
My heart will sing Your praise again
Jesus, You're still enough
Keep me within Your love
My heart will sing Your praise again

[Chorus]

Your promise still stands
Great is Your faithfulness, faithfulness
I'm still in Your hands
This is my confidence, You've never failed
Your promise still stands
Great is Your faithfulness, faithfulness
I'm still in Your hands
This is my confidence, You've never failed me yet [25]

As I've learned more about the origins of this song, it starts out from the book of Joshua. But, I knew as we sang, and confirmed as I researched it, that Lamentations 3 played a big role in the writing of this song.

Similarly, one of the most popular hymns in history comes from Lamentations 3. *"Great is Thy Faithfulness"*. I became familiar with this song as a child while playing matchbox cars and drawing pictures on the offering envelopes while laying underneath the pew at church each Sunday morning. It wasn't until years later that these words truly landed on me. These words come directly out of the "Yet". A remembrance that He is faithful and His mercies are new to you and I each morning.

I would encourage you to take a moment right now to worship. Maybe you are reading alone and can sing. Maybe you are in public and have a voice like mine and feel that it's best that you sing in your head. Either way, whether you sing or speak, take a few moments to simply worship God by proclaiming His faithfulness.

How has God been faithful to you in the past? Spend some time writing out God's past faithfulness to you personally.

_____

_____

_____

_____

_____

I would encourage you to daily cling to God's faithfulness to you in the past. Be reminded of His goodness toward you in past times so that when difficulty strikes, it's at the forefront of your mind that He has been faithful and He will be again. That's a promise you can grab hold of!

LIVING WITH HOPE

We have talked so much about moving forward with hope. But what is hope? Like, real, Biblical hope?

> "...biblical hope is not just a desire for something good in the future, but rather, biblical hope is a confident expectation and desire for something good in the future. Biblical hope not only desires something good for the future; it expects it to happen. And it not only expects it to happen; it is confident that it will happen. There is a moral certainty that the good we expect and desire will be done." **-John Piper** [26]

Do you remember what Jeremiah said in Lamentations 3 right after he poured out his heart in regards to how miserable and lacking in peace he was? Do you remember his response after the "yet"?

> "Yet I still dare to hope when I remember this:" [27]
> **Lamentations 3:21 (NLT)**

The main point of "yet", as we've discussed throughout the book, is finding hope in the midst of pain. Why? We see Jeremiah remembering God's faithfulness, goodness, mercy, love, and presence with him. And when he's reminded of God, he hopes. As the song *Do It Again* states, "You've never failed me yet". And so, even in moments of the most extreme pain, Christians can remind themselves that God has never failed them and never will. We can be reminded of just how faithful He is. And because of that truth, we're reminded of the hope we have. This is amazing! Jeremiah then goes on in verse 24 to say:

> *I say to myself, "The Lord is my inheritance; therefore, I will hope in him!"* [28]

Did you hear that? Because of the Lord, he has hope. There is nothing that can bring you and I any level of hope in the midst of grief or in life in general. It is ALL about Jesus. There is no hope to be found without Him!

Jeremiah says that the Lord is his inheritance. Reader, if you are in Christ, He is your inheritance as well. He is what you receive now and He is what you receive for eternity. He's the greatest blessing there is, and we get Him. THEREFORE, we have hope in Him, just as Jeremiah did. Jeremiah knew in his head and experienced with his heart the faithfulness of God, so when difficulty struck, he clung to the truth that he understood and experienced!

Because of the life, death, and resurrection of Jesus, we have hope! Hope for the moment and hope for the future.

We have this hope because we know that whatever may come against us in this life, whatever trials we face, whatever grief has broken our hearts, we have eternity with Jesus Christ awaiting us. And, not just eternity, we have life on this earth with Jesus, in which He has given us His Holy Spirit. If you love Jesus, you have Him now and for eternity. What an incredible hope!

If you are a Christian, you believe that all things will one day be redeemed, right? We cling to the redemptive work of Christ. By living this out, the loss you've experienced and the heartbreak that goes with it, as difficult as it may be, is not going to last forever. Some things God chooses to redeem while we're still on this earth, and then all others are redeemed in Glory. It is His promise that He will redeem all things. In the end, Jesus wins, and we will experience that in ways our minds cannot even begin to fathom. In one tangible way that we can begin to understand though, is that there will be no more death, no more grief, no more crying, no more pain, no more difficulty, no more of what you are currently experiencing. That will be taken away completely. Do you believe that? This is a promise from God. Cling to it!

> *He will wipe away every tear from their eyes. Death will be no more; grief, crying, and pain will be no more, because the previous things have passed away.*
> **-Revelation 21:4 (CSB)** [29]

But just because we believe that Heaven is in our future and all things will be made right again, does not mean that your grief is less important, or shouldn't be experienced. We grieve because our hearts long for perfection. Our hearts long for what once was and what will someday be again. Our hearts long for no sin, no death, no pain, no suffering, no grief. So it's OK to grieve. But it's also OK to look ahead with hope in what is to come. It's OK to allow the joy of salvation overwhelm your heart even as you hurt. Both can happen simultaneously.

Living with hope doesn't mean you have to stop grieving. I miss my mother-in-law terribly, and, as I write this, we are preparing to visit San Diego and all of Cathie's family... all but one. It breaks my heart that we won't see her there. It breaks my heart that she won't enjoy Disneyland with her grandkids. It breaks my heart that I won't get to hear her shriek with excitement when we get to her front door. But, at the same time, I'm reminded that we WILL see her again. We will have that moment of greeting in Glory and I hope I get to hear that shriek of excitement again! We will have way better experiences together than Disney could ever hope to provide us. So, while my heart hurts, I continue to look forward, where Christ will make all things right again. That's the hope He has provided us.

Christian, you may be in a place where you've lost hope. Maybe you've pulled back from Jesus. Or, maybe you've just lost perspective. Maybe you've become so blinded by your grief that you've forgotten what you have in Jesus. Be reminded of who He is, what He has done, and what He is doing. There is a day coming, friend, when you will embrace your savior. Now THAT is hope that we can all cling to!

What you have endured and what you are currently enduring is so hard. Stay mindful of who He is and who you are in Him. Stay mindful of what lies ahead for you in eternity. Stay mindful that His Holy Spirit is with you now, and even in difficult times, this life is His and you are here to serve Him. Difficult times will come and go. There will be more loss in your life. And yet, He will continue to be faithful to you, leading you to eternity with Him. Keep Him in the crosshairs of your life and your hope can never be shaken! This hope of eternity, where Christ redeems all things, is coming. That's His promise to us and it's going to be amazing! That day is coming. Do you believe it?

For I consider that the sufferings of this present time are not worth comparing with the glory that is going to be revealed to us.
-Romans 8:18 (CSB) [30]

2 In my Father's house are many rooms; if not, I would have told you. I am going away to prepare a place for you. 3 If I go away and prepare a place for you, I will come again and take you to myself, so that where I am you may be also. 4 You know the way to where I am going."
-John 14:2-4 (CSB) [31]

"Look, I am coming soon"
-Revelation 22:12a (CSB) [32]

Write out the hope you have in Jesus. How do these scriptures encourage your heart right now? Speak this hope to God in worship as you write.

_____

_____

_____

_____

_____

In the introduction, I shared with you many of the times I have grieved over the years. One of those experiences was with a family that we consider dear friends. Fred and Hope and their daughters McKalyn and Maddie were long time neighbors of ours in Ohio. We had bought my grandparents house next door to these dear friends, so I grew up around them when at my grandparent's house as a kid, and then became their neighbors, and more importantly, friends.

On Christmas Eve of 2007, Fred and Hope's oldest daughter, Hollis, was with her boyfriend and his family at a family get-together. Later that evening, while driving home, someone pulled out in front of them. Hollis was thrown from the vehicle and she did not survive. Her boyfriend, Elliott, who was a star football player in our town, had a severely injured shoulder that would require surgery. Elliott's brother, Brock, was paralyzed. The boys' father, Dave, also passed away. This story may sound familiar to you, as it was highlighted often on ESPN over the years because of Elliot's football career and Brock walking again after being given a one percent chance to ever do so.

Just like that, on what is the happiest and most hope-filled evening each year in celebration of the coming of Christ, two parents are suddenly without a daughter. Two little girls without their big sister. I'm sure this is triggering some difficult memories for you as you read this, but I share their story though because it's a story of hope! Truly, and I've witnessed it first hand, this family is the greatest model of "yet" that I've ever personally witnessed in my life.

Fred and Hope still grieve Hollis' passing. They miss their daughter so much. Each time we talk about her, I see the tears well up in their eyes as they give a smile that says, "God is good, but I miss my daughter." In the midst of their grief, and without knowing it, this family has modeled "yet" for me and so many others over the years. They have grieved heavily, and yet, their trust in Jesus has been unwavering, for all four of them.

This is a family that trusted Jesus before losing Hollis, and so, when Hollis passed away, they knew of God's faithfulness and they clung to it. It hasn't been easy. Actually, far from it. This family has endured so much heartache. They've grieved hard, and rightfully so. But, they've not wavered in clinging to Jesus. It has certainly been difficult at times, but they've continually chosen to live in the "Yet", and I'm so thankful that they have!

I had the opportunity to interview this family for an Easter video we were creating at my former church years ago. I asked Fred, Hope, McKalyn, and Maddie to share their hope because of the resurrection of Christ. Here are some snippets of that interview:

Hope (mom): *Knowing that He's alive, that He rose again, it gives us purpose. Because, I know that my daughter...her body died, but her spirit is in Heaven.*

Fred (dad): *For me, it's an assurance that in the end we do win as believers. And, to me, that's...wow!*

McKalyn: *It gives me a purpose to live every single day, because without that hope, what are we here for? It allows me to get through each day knowing that there's a light at the end of the tunnel. This is not my home and I have an eternal home with Jesus Christ.*

Maddie: *On those difficult days, it's just taking a second to sit there and think about it and say, "OK, I know He rose again and I know that my sister is with Him in Heaven. For me, it's that idea that I know I get to see her again someday, I know I get to be with my Savior in Heaven, so I can make it through this day or these next weeks or whatever I'm struggling with." For me, it's the joy that I know I will experience someday.*

McKalyn: *I feel like peace is something I have experienced so much through this process, and the thing is, it's only a peace that He can give. You cannot feel this sense of peace when you experience loss or pain in any way. There's only a peace that comes through Jesus Christ and believing in Him, and if you don't have that, then I don't know how you can get through it fully, and really heal without that.*

When asked to finish the sentence, "I would give any-thing to _____", the girls responded like this:

McKalyn: *I would give anything to have my sister at my wedding, but there is a God and He's alive, and because I have that hope, I know that my sister, because she was a believer, is right there with Him. And so, I don't feel like she won't be present on my big day. Having that hope, I feel that I can go through that day and know that she might not by physically standing there, but because of my hope in Jesus Christ, be-cause I know she is with Him, I can fully enjoy that day.*

Maddie: *I wish she could be there for your (McKalyn's) wedding and my wedding and my graduation and see me go to college and all that stuff. But for me, I think the Lord has given me a peace that I will see her again and even though it really stinks not having her here in real life to enjoy these happy moments with us, I know that I have something to look forward to and it's gonna be awesome!*

SIDE NOTE: This family spoke of knowing they'd see Hollis again. You may be grieving the loss of someone who did not know Christ and you're confident that they are not with Jesus and you will not see them again. For this, I am so sorry. Losing a loved one who did not know Jesus can take grief to deeper levels because there isn't the hope of seeing them again. However, our ultimate hope lies in Jesus and our eternity with Him. When it comes to our loved ones and "where they are," we cannot seek to find our hope in seeing them again. Christ is our treasure, both on this earth and for eternity. Trust Him with your heart as you wrestle through these difficult thoughts regarding your loved ones.

HIS GRACE GIVES HOPE

Our God is a God of grace. Because of the work of Jesus and our trust in Him, He promises us eternity with Him, sharing in His Glory. This is our hope! In the meantime, while on this earth, we are going to endure hardship. If you are reading this now, you're living it. That hardship, difficulty and grief develop endurance in our hearts. Now, if you're like me, you're thinking, "but I'd prefer not to learn or endure anything through this season. I just want _____ back." None of us would prefer to be in this place. We are though, so what do we do? We endure, which develops character. And what does character do? It strengthens our hope! And, as we live with hope, we are constantly reminded of just how much God loves us! And, most important in all of this, is that He has given those who trust and love Him His Holy Spirit! Spend some time sitting in this scripture and responding to it:

> *2 Because of our faith, Christ has brought us into this place of undeserved privilege where we now stand, and we confidently and joyfully look forward to sharing God's glory. 3 We can rejoice, too, when we run into problems and trials, for we know that they help us develop endurance. 4 And endurance develops strength of character, and character strengthens our confident hope of salvation. 5 And this hope will not lead to disappointment. For we know how dearly God loves us,*

because he has given us the Holy Spirit to fill our
hearts with his love.
 - Romans 5:2-5 (NLT) [33]

With how much confidence and joy do you look forward to sharing God's glory? Explain.

_____

_____

_____

_____

_____

How have you grown in endurance and how has your
character been developed in this season of grief? Explain.

_____

_____

_____

_____

_____

Verse 5 says that we know how dearly God loves us. Do
you? How have you experienced His love in the midst of
your grief? How has His love for you changed the way you
grieve?

_____

_____

_____

_____

_____

Our hope is in what Jesus has done, is doing, and will do. Our hope lies in nothing that we do or say or accomplish. It is ALL by the work of Jesus and our trust in Him. Our hope lies in the eternal future we have with Him. Nothing, and I mean, nothing can steal our hope in what is ahead for those who trust in Him. Let's spend some time in Revelation 21:3-4, where we see what we have to look forward to, and then respond to the Lord in worship...

> **3** *I heard a loud shout from the throne, saying, "Look, God's home is now among his people! He will live with them, and they will be his people. God himself will be with them.* **4** *He will wipe every tear from their eyes, and there will be no more death or sorrow or crying or pain. All these things are gone forever."*
> - **Revelation 21:3-4 (NLT)** [34]

Write out, in worship, what Jesus has done, is doing, and will do that gives you hope in this moment.

_____

_____

_____

_____

_____

GIVEN A NEW PERSPECTIVE IN THE "YET"

When we moved to the Nashville area in the summer of 2017, Josh and Christi were some of the first people we connected with, and they continue to be some of our dearest friends (Check out their work at famousathome.com. It's life-changing!). We learned in our first conversation that Josh's dad passed away within a month of when Cathie's mom had passed away the previous fall. There was an immediate grief connection. Needless to say, we were all still heartbroken over the loss of a parent we so dearly love.

I'd like to close this chapter by sharing Josh's story of his dad and how his passing has changed them as they continue to live in the "yet".

Growing up, my dad taught me to play baseball, took me to Penn State football games, and spent countless hours in the backyard with me playing every game imaginable. Even our collection of baseball cards is a memory forever etched into my soul. I was living every child's dream of having a great dad.

Then, in 1993, at the ripe young age of 34, my dad got sick. Really sick. What started as the common cold somehow turned into two weeks in the hospital, the second of which was spent at a more sophisticated hospital for cardiac patients. My dad had been diagnosed with congestive heart failure.

At 13, I was guarded from the details. However, I do remember my mom and stepdad taking me to the river one weekend to get my mind off of things. My lone memory during those two weeks was a night fishing excursion on the river where I laid on the bottom of a boat bawling, worried about whether my dad was going to live.

Fortunately, he survived. And though my dad was unable to run and limited in how active he could be, he did really well on medication for the next ten years, and we continued making more and more memories together. Truth be told, other than not being as physical, not much else had changed for us. We still threw baseball, shot hoops, and went to sporting events. As a wrestler in high school, I can count on one hand the number of wrestling matches my dad missed. He was always in the stands.

But in 2003, something shifted. At his ten-year checkup, my dad's cardiologist told him that he could write a book because he hadn't expected him to be doing so well, let alone be alive.

His cardiologist's words came as a shock to me, eliminating any illusion I held of invincibility. I think my dad continued to hold details of his health from me. I had no idea my dad's heart was in such bad shape.

Being in graduate school and living away from home, I started asking more questions. The more I learned, the more grateful I became, not just for my dad, but also for our extended time together. God used his cardiologist's words to change how I viewed our time together. My dad's congestive heart failure had become a gift.

That same year, I decided to start what would become an annual tradition—a Phillies baseball game for Father's Day.

No matter where my job or life took me in the years that followed, we always made it to our Phillies game. I'm convinced this tradition would not have started if not for my dad being diagnosed with congestive heart failure.

Even living a few hours apart, I took the reins of making sure we made the most of every moment we had together. I didn't want to take any moment for granted.

Yet, I carried many fears. My greatest fear was losing my dad. I wanted him to meet his grandchildren, watch them grow up, and be there for their celebrations, just as he was there for me. I also grew quite worried because he became complacent in his faith. Though we had a deep connection with sports, our faith conversations stayed on the surface. I prayed countless hours for him to come to see the God of universe in a life-changing way.

MY PRAYERS ANSWERED

Then, in 2014, I received that phone call—the kind that leaves your legs weak and your stomach churning. My dad was now critical. His heart, on its own, officially failed. The left chamber was no longer able to pump blood into his organs. They too were shutting down.

In the next frantic and stressed three hours, with no planes available until the next day, we decided to pack the family into the car and drive the 17 hours from Missouri to Pennsylvania to be with him. My wife, Christi, is a hero. In the midst of the unknowns and all of the emotions and *illogical thinking that accompanies it, she packed up all of the belongings for our six-week-old daughter, two-year-old son, and herself, and bravely stepped foot into the car for the next 17 hours through the night—all for the sake of helping my dad through the toughest battle of his life.*

With 30 minutes of sleep in a 42 hour span and a drive half-way across the country, we arrived in Hershey, Pennsylvania in time to see my dad coming out of surgery where he received a heart pump (aka LVAD) to do the work of the left chamber for him.

Three days after he received his first heart pump we were sitting together in the ICU and he said to me, "When I first was diagnosed 23 years ago I asked God to allow me to see you kids grow up. Now I'm asking Him for a bonus—to enjoy my grandkids."

Little did we know, the next two years were filled with blood clots, long hospital stays and three heart pump surgeries. Yes, you read that correctly. Three heart pumps. Three times he had his chest opened. Three times he had to go through rehab. Watching him persevere through those times was the proudest and saddest I had ever been. Holding both emotions was difficult. He lived in pain everyday, fighting for his family.

But even more, God was answering my prayers. My dad confided in me about encounters he had on the operating table that enlivened his soul. Our faith conversation started dominating our sports conversation.

For the next two years, and for each one of those surgeries, he had a wooden cross he held in his hand, affectionately becoming known by the nurses and doctors in the hospital as the man who carried the cross.

I like to think that congestive heart failure was the cross he carried. But the grace with which he carried it left us all with memories that challenged us to look beyond this momentary life.

My dad's precarious health condition taught me the value of a moment. The gift of a conversation shared. The gift of time spent together.

Jesus told us not to be anxious about our lives...because, could being anxious add a single hour to a person's life?"

And now that I'm a dad, I ask myself, "Which of you by being anxious can add more joy to the moments he shares with his kids?"

Not promised tomorrow, moments matter. My dad was the master of making the most of moments.

Anytime we were visiting Pennsylvania in those two tumultuous years, facing life without my dad, I often grieved by driving through the hills of Pennsylvania, past the places where many of our memories were made—the sights, smells, and sounds that brought me face-to-face with the lessons he taught me throughout my childhood years. What's amazing about those lessons is that every one of them were a result of what he did, not what he said. By being present in the good times and bad, and simply showing me how much I was loved.

LITTLE WARNING

October 22nd, 2016. *Christi, my wife, was out of town visiting her grandparents in Canada. That meant just me with the kids—Landon, 4 and Kennedy, 2— for the weekend. We spent the day at a local pumpkin patch. Going down slides. Trekking through a corn maze. Riding on a wagon through the woods. And of course, texting pictures to my Dad.*

Weekends in the fall remind me of him. Playing football together in the backyard. Going to Penn State football games. Tailgating with apples and caramel dip outside Beaver Stadium.

Not surprisingly, I dressed our family in Penn State blue and white for the pumpkin patch. That evening, Ohio State would be entering Beaver Stadium in what's become known as a "white out." Once the kids were down, Dad and I would be watching the game together through text and phone calls.

However, on this particular day, his phone call came earlier than expected.

"Josh," he said, "I'm not feeling well and the numbers on my heart pump are high. Deb (my stepmom) is taking me to Hershey [Medical Center]."

Dad had been in and out of the hospital every so often since receiving three heart pumps in a six-month span beginning in September 2014. Blood clots going through the pump were the usual culprit—and the reason he had so many heart pumps replaced in such a short time.

But this last heart pump seemed to chew up and spit out blood clots like a ball player with sunflower seeds. Unfortunately, it seemed to make these hospital visits for a blood clot in his pump eerily routine.

After a number of text messages letting me know he was in the emergency room, I received this text at 8:17 PM EST, shortly after kickoff.

"My MAP came down to 93 but I'm just laying here. They are going to keep me. Still did not see my cardiologist but the doctor in the ER said they are keeping me."

That text was followed up by this one: "What is the score, I have no TV in this room."

You mean to tell me he's at Penn State Hershey Medical Center and he can't watch the Penn State game? During the next two hours I kept Dad updated on the first three quarters.

Then, he sent me this: "Going to room 1171."

Dad was in the hospital for what we thought might be a blood clot in his heart pump. I know it sounds serious, because it is. But this was the man whose cardiologist told him he could write a book at the ten-year mark.

Now, 23 years after his initial diagnosis, Ironman—as we affectionately called him—lay in the hospital, yet again.

Maybe I was just in denial, but I don't think so. I think I genuinely came to believe he was going to make it through anything. Dad's will to live was unmatched.

With little warning, that would be the last text message I received from my Dad.

THE GIFTED WARNING

One of the mementos in my office today is a picture of my Dad and I sitting at Harry the K's restaurant, overlooking Citizens Bank Park at one of our Phillies games. I remember that day very well. We always made the most of the time we had at the park.

One time, we even attended a double header against the Tigers, deciding to stay for both games.

At another game, while watching batting practice from the outfield, it began a torrential downpour. We got soaked. But man, did we laugh. That was one of my favorite moments.

A few years prior to that game, we drove my grandma's car the 2 ½ hour drive to Philadelphia. On the way there the car began to overheat. Every so often we had to pull off the highway to allow the engine to cool down. Though it took a little longer than usual, we weren't missing our game.

The drive home that night was hot and loud. We kept the heat on high—and the windows down—to help keep the engine, and ourselves, from overheating until we got home. The laughter, and sweat, filled the car.

Come to think of it, I had more warning in my life than I realized.

Those mementos, beginning in 2003, were our gift—a prized reminder that life is short.

A gift we made the most of.

THE GAME

As it turns out, it was Dad's will to live, not his heart pump, that made him Ironman. This heart pump was damaged. And Dad was just too weak to go through another heart pump surgery. Not only that, looking back on it, I believe he came to know intimately the beauty of real life on the other side.

On November 5th, 2016, two weeks after entering the hospital, Dad walked into the arms of Jesus. Holding his hand, reading Romans 8, and praying him into heaven is one of the most bittersweet moments of my life.

There's not a day that goes by that I don't think of Dad. Sometimes I look at those sporting mementos and I cry. I cry hard. Other times I look at them and just laugh.

In the years since his death, I believe wholeheartedly that what he imparted to me upon entering heaven is a vision of the "yet".

Holding a Ph.D. and having a seminary degree doesn't make your understanding of heaven any more clear than the next person. I found in the months following my dad's death that my mind often wandered to what my dad is doing now, who he's with, what he knows, what he's doing.

Part of my grief process in the years that followed was to find out. I devoured books about heaven. I wanted a glimpse of hope in the midst of my tears. If you haven't noticed already, I grieve by experiencing the nostalgic moments built around our time together—the places, the smells, the sounds, the tastes, and the cool fall football air.

Studying heaven gave me permission to dream about what it will be like when we reunite with our loved ones. When my dad gets to hold his grandkids in his arms. When we all get to play baseball in the backyard together again. When we can laugh and experience those sensory moments in perfect harmony, together.

Not only do I believe my dad imparted to me a passion for the new earth when he "crossed over," I also believe through a powerful prophetic word that he summoned angels to protect our family in the way he had hoped to after he departed earth. I could go into more detail on this, but it's too special a testimony to have it be criticized by others as being too sensational. Some memories, we need to just hold tight to not be corrupted.

Instead, I'll use the words of Richard Rolheiser in his book Sacred Fire to explain what my dad left behind, "Like Jesus," Rolheiser writes, "we can really send our spirits only after we go away."

Rolheiser goes on to explain, "We experience this everywhere we go in life: a grown child has to leave home before her parents can fully understand and appreciate her for who she is. There comes a day in a young person's life when she stands before her parents and, in whatever way she articulates it, says the words: 'It is better for you that I go away! Unless I go, you will never really know who I am. You will have some heartache now, but that pain will eventually become warm because I will come back to you in a deeper way.'" 35

My dad came back to me in a deeper way. Through his

death, he left me with a vision for the afterlife we impart on our children and imagine to this day.

Just as I experienced every sweet moment with my dad, what I now experience in my heart, not by intellect alone, is that the Bible ends with Jesus "making all things new."

That's the hope we live for, that Jesus is making "all things new."

We live in such a way that that future "yet" we talk about brings the Lord's Prayer to life for us in the here and now--"on earth as it is in heaven." The "yet", for us, is seeing what God is doing NOW and wants to do in us and through us. However, it took my dad's death for me to experience it in a new, more tangible way. To literally see God making all things new right now. And that He invites us into that is what we're teaching our kids. That it's not just about salvation and getting to go to heaven, but that it's about being a child of God and bringing heaven to earth right now for the sake of others and His glory.

Though I find solace in knowing that I will see Dad again one day, it in no way takes away the pain I experience as a son who misses his father.

Natural death is brutal.

Death separates you from all of the moments. All of the life. All of the laughter.

All of the downpours together.

All of the times you sit along the road just waiting for the engine to cool down.

All of the apples and caramel dip while tailgating.

All of the pumpkin patches.

All of the times you want to pick up the phone and just talk.

But the game goes on. *And what I'm learning through my own grief is that the more you embrace the tears, the more you have in you to embrace the laughter.*

Don't miss out on the moments. We're all on a timeline. Enjoying the game.

But preparing our hearts for the fully embodied, "Yet."

"Tears are permitted, but they must glisten in the light of faith and hope." [36]
-**Charles Spurgeon**

Respond to these words from Charles Spurgeon. What do they do to you? How does it encourage or challenge your heart in this moment?

_____

_____

_____

_____

_____

CHAPTER 5

HE'S FAITHFUL & PRESENT

G rief is lonely. It's one thing when we feel let down by those who failed to show up during this season, but it's another level of loneliness when we perceive God to be absent, or worse, that He may not care. Let me assure you, He both is present with you right now in this second and He cares so much for you. He cares more deeply than even you do. He cares for you and He loves you. Your circumstances in life aren't a reflection of His love for you.

Although your circumstances are difficult, it does not mean God has abandoned you. The opposite, really. He's fully present with you if you have surrendered your life to Him. As we talked about earlier, it's still easy for us as followers of Jesus to cry out things like, "Where are you? Are you sleeping? Do you even care?" He promises His presence, and God always keeps His promises. Jeremiah 29 has a really popular verse that is often taken out of context. We often hear Jeremiah 29:11 in a twisted form, because people like to think that God's goal is to prosper us. Verse 11 is great, in context, but I so wish that people would grab ahold of and use verses 12-14 just as much on social media posts, tattoos, and wall art for their kid's bedroom.

> **12** *In those days when you pray, I will listen.* **13** *If you look for me wholeheartedly, you will find me.* **14** *I will be found by you," says the Lord.*
> **-Jeremiah 29:12-14a (NLT)** [37]

We see God promise basically the same thing, three times over.

> **Promise #1:** When you pray, I will listen.
> **Promise #2:** If you look for me wholeheartedly, you will find me.
> **Promise #3:** I will be found by you.

All three promises are His presence to those whose eyes are fixed on Him. You aren't alone and He has not forgotten you. Remember earlier when we talked about 2 Chronicles 20:12?

> *We do not know what to do, but our eyes are on you.*
> **- 2 Chronicles 20:12, The MSG Translation** [38]

If our response to Jesus in the midst of our grief is this, then we know because of His promise that He responds with, "Here I am".

Are you praying and feeling like he's not hearing you?

Are you looking for Him and feeling like you've come up empty-handed? Do you feel like this is a giant game of hide-and-go-seek and He went and hid and you're still stumped on where He is? Feeling this way is OK, and as we talked earlier, tell Him you feel that way. Do you feel like He's asleep and doesn't care about your situation? Tell Him! But, what we cannot do is say that He isn't present. If you are trusting Jesus and seeking after Him, He's promised you His presence.

David writes in Psalm 34:

> 4 I prayed to the Lord, and he answered me. He freed me from all my fears. 5 Those who look to him for help will be radiant with joy; no shadow of shame will darken their faces. 6 In my desperation I prayed, and the Lord listened; he saved me from all my troubles. 7 For the angel of the Lord is a guard; he surrounds and defends all who fear him. 8 Taste and see that the Lord is good. Oh, the joys of those who take refuge in him!
> 17 The Lord hears his people when they call to him for help. He rescues them from all their troubles. 18 The Lord is close to the brokenhearted; he rescues those whose spirits are crushed.
> **-Psalm 34:4-8, 17-18 (NLT)** [39]

It is obvious as we read throughout the Psalms that David's life was not an easy one. He faced a significant amount of hardship (some out of his control, and some that he directly caused). However, we read verse 5, in which he says, *"Those who look to him for help will be radiant with joy; no shadow of shame will darken their faces."* [40] David praised God in the midst of difficulty because throughout his life he had "tasted and seen that the Lord is good". He had a personal relationship with God and He rested in God's love. So, when David was in a bad way and needed help, he poured his heart out to God and God responded. If you've experienced God's love and faithfulness, you will be reminded of Him as you face difficulty. That remembrance will bring you to a place of peace and hope.

How have you personally tasted and seen that the Lord is good in the midst of your grief?

_____

_____

_____

_____

_____

There was an older woman in my previous church who, while having recently lost her husband, was also battling a number of serious health issues. Life was hard. While visiting with her one day, I asked her what kept her so joyful and so hopeful while grieving her husband's passing and also battling her own serious physical ailments. She responded by quoting scripture. She responded by saying, "God said:

> *Don't be afraid, for I am with you. Don't be discouraged, for I am your God. I will strengthen you*

and help you. I will hold you up with my victorious right hand.
-Isaiah 41:10 (NLT) [41]

I loved her response! Because, like David, she spoke of God's goodness and promises IN THE MIDST OF difficulty and grief. These promises from God just stuck with me, because when times are hard, these are the things we can and should cling to when we are in a difficult place. These are the words we can remind ourselves of when we're struggling. These are the truths to grab hold of when we're instead grabbing hold of the lies of the evil one.

So, let's break this scripture down.

God says: "Don't be afraid." Not, "Don't be afraid, if..." Just simply, "Don't be afraid." It's here that we get more promises from God to cling to! Why shouldn't I be afraid?

• **Promise #1:** I am with you.

God says: "Don't be discouraged." Not, "Don't be discouraged, if...". Just simply, "Don't be discouraged." Why shouldn't I be discouraged?

• **Promise (and reminder) #2:** I am your God.

God continues on with more promises:

• **Promise #3:** I will strengthen you.
• **Promise #4:** I will help you.

• **Promise #5:** I will hold you up with my victorious right hand.

These are the promises of a faithful God to His people that He loves dearly. This is for you. So, in those moments of fear, loneliness, weakness, sadness, and even lacking faith, be reminded of His words. He is present with you, right now. He is at work in you, right now. He has the victory already and is holding you up with His mighty and victorious hand. He is protecting you, right now. Trust Him. Grab hold of this truth and don't let go!

TRUSTING HIS PROMISES

Life was good and soon to be better for Felipe and Michelle. They had 6 kids with a 7th on the way in just a few months. On this chilly winter week in Ohio, some of the family had come down with the flu, passing it around to one another. Ava, their seven-year-old daughter, had come down with this sickness and it seemed to hit her harder than the others. Late that night, they felt the need to take Ava to the hospital, as her condition worsened. While being treated for influenza A, Ava's health continued to decline. The next morning, as an absolute shock to everyone, precious little Ava passed away. This healthy and active little girl who loved to dance, was gone. No warning, no time to prepare, no chance to say goodbye. In what felt like the blink of an eye, there was a family, a group of friends, a school, and a community that was absolutely traumatized as they entered into this deep and gut-wrenching grief.

As Cathie and I sat in their living room that evening, I saw mourning in a way I never had before, and I thought I'd seen it all. I'd been in over a hundred funerals, walked through bereavement with countless numbers of people, was present with dozens of families while standing around their loved one as they passed. For the first time in my life, I experienced what I'd always hoped I wouldn't ever have to. The death of a young child. This moment left an entire family reeling as they sat motionless on their couch together. They were in shock. Unable to wrap their minds around what just happened, and certainly without the capacity to look ahead to the future without little Ava. It's a tragedy like this that makes one think, "*This stuff happens to other people. These are the things you hear about on the news. This doesn't happen in your own home.*" For Felipe and Michelle, it did. They were thrown into the pit of grief without any notice. Our hearts were completely broken for them and I knew leaving the house that night how badly they needed to find the hope that can only be found in Jesus Christ. Sure, they believed in God, but there wasn't yet a complete trust in Jesus. They'd now be the first people to tell you this.

Little did we all know that evening the journey God was about to take them on. A journey of coming to find their everything in Him. It's been a hard journey. One they would never choose, and yet, a journey they wouldn't trade because of the hope they now have in Christ Jesus. Does it continue to be hard for this family? Absolutely! They miss

Ava like crazy and every day is a reminder that she's no longer with them them. I'd like for you to hear from Michelle how God has worked in their hearts over these years...

Our grief experience:

On February 7, 2017 we unexpectedly lost our 7 year old daughter Ava after she fell ill with Influenza A. I layed with her and held her until it happened. I screamed, I prayed, and I collapsed to the ground. I passed out, being 6 months pregnant, and I woke up in labor and delivery. I will never forget the look on my husband's pale face as he walked into that room. Together we went back up to her room and held our baby to say goodbye. As I laid my head on her I felt an indescribable feeling of peace over my body. It wasn't until later that I realized that was from God.

When we began moving forward:

I remember after the funeral just laying and unable to move, trying to process how I would go on and how I would ever be able to live again. We had a community who rallied together and lifted me up and carried me though when I couldn't stand. God was working in people's hearts and I knew it was Him helping me. Every day I was blown away by more food than we could ever eat, money that allowed my husband to be home with us during this awful time, gifts, books, it was amazing! We felt so loved! The anonymous letters saying "God laid you on my heart. I felt the nudge to send you this." I clung to all of It and I needed it. I couldn't bear to walk back in our church where Ava's funeral was. I was scared of any reminder of those awful days. I was striving for answers. I read the Bible and any other book with scripture. It was the same Bible I had always read but it was different now. There was a change in my heart as I read it. I was searching for any answer, any piece of comfort to get me through that hour. It was all I did and my husband began to do the same. I realized nothing else was good enough to fill that void. Nothing else could fill my heart again other than God and His word and His promises. When I wanted to be angry and focus on the negative, He would send someone my way every single time. He made sure I knew He was there with me. I started to realize God did not take her away to hurt me and I had to trust Him, just the way I had before. He is the only way. Day by day I felt more peace and God continued to show me the way. He is amazing and I watched His perfect timing help heal us.

Our response to the Lord in the midst of grief:

I went through many stages of grief. Day to day, minute to minute...it was a rollercoaster ride of emotions. When I took my eyes off of the Lord and focused on my broken heart, I fell into a dark place of sadness. I realized after many panic attacks and hospital visits for stress ulcers in my stomach, that I was getting nowhere. If God's word starting my day set me up for a good day, then why not keep my focus there? Even though the triggers, the holidays, the heart breaks, I had to keep my eyes on God. I gave it all to Him. I am still learning and He is showing me the way.

How we've experienced God's faithfulness:

Looking back, His faithfulness has been nothing short of amazing. The love, support and timing will blow you away. I have sat back and thought, "thank you Lord, I needed just that." From sitting in the car or on the couch crying and getting a message from a friend or phone call saying "I love you. Can I pray with you?" Just God's perfect timing that leaves you sitting there in awe. Our Pastor seeming to know just what we were struggling with every Sunday. A kiss from Heaven. God knows, and if you just be still, He will show you.

Growing trust:

My faith is stronger than ever before and my relationship with God is amazing. He is truly all we

*have and He is so good to us. I have felt the worst
pain possible in this life by losing a child, and
because of Him, I see purpose. He has made bad
good and used my family to show many His faithfulness. However, it took me a while to see this.*

A word for the grieving:

*The one and only thing to get you though this
is God. Keep your eyes and heart on Him. Even
through the anger and tears, He will restore you.
I never thought I would make it this far, as awful
as that is to say. I promise He will show you the
way. He has conquered the grave. He is the light
and the truth. Open your heart to Him and He
will forever change you.*

My prayer is that what Michelle has shared would be an
encouragement to you in the midst of your own journey.
Every day is hard, and yet this family is choosing to trust
Jesus. That doesn't take away the pain and it doesn't make
them miss sweet Ava any less. What I absolutely love about
this family is that they've lived out, "*We do not know what to
do, but our eyes are on you.*" (2 Chronicles 20:12, The MSG)
[42]. They knew God's promises and they chose to trust Him
as they grieved. They trusted that God was present with
them, and as they trusted Him, He changed their hearts!
This family can now move forward in grief because they
KNOW God is good, present and faithful.

Maybe you are reading this and wishing your heart was able to respond to God in the way that Felipe and Michelle's has. Maybe you haven't fully believed that God is with you in the midst of this season. Maybe you used to believe that until things all came crashing down, and now you are left wondering if everything you've ever believed is a lie. It's not uncommon to question God's goodness in the midst of grief. But if you aren't confident in who God is in both the good times and bad, your grief is going to be difficult.

I have a friend who has not only experienced the loss of those he loves, but has also endured a number of difficult life circumstances that has left him questioning God's goodness. As a Christian the majority of his life, he would tell you that God is good. But when extreme difficulty hit, he began to lose confidence that God was with him and for him. He began to lose confidence that God loved both he and those around him. He began to question God's faithfulness to him, almost as if God had forgotten or abandoned him.

My friend's grief and suffering has become almost unbearable. It's completely overwhelmed him. Why? He's stopped trusting in God's goodness and faithfulness to Him. He is no longer certain that God loves him. While he would still call himself a Christian, he lives as if God doesn't care for Him like he does for others who are experiencing what he would call a "good life".

That is no way to live! Let me rephrase: That is an awful way to live! Why? Because it's not true! God is for you. God is with you. God delights in you. He is faithful to you. He is merciful toward you. He loves you. Your life circumstances do not define His character. As we've discussed, you have to remind yourself of this. The evil one wants nothing more than for you to grieve without hope. He wants you to forget or ignore God's love for you and His goodness toward you. You can be certain of this. It's never a question. Hear this: God loves you. God is faithful to you. God is trustworthy. Cling to these truths!

The Lord your God is among you, a warrior who saves. He will rejoice over you with gladness. He will be quiet in his love. He will delight in you with singing."
- **Zephaniah 3:17 (CSB)** [43]

God is with you and loves you and delights in you. It's a basic, and yet overwhelmingly incredible truth of being a Christian. It's one of the first things Christian parents teach their kids. You know this truth and you've obviously heard this truth. I'm also going to assume that you believe this truth. And yet, I'm sure there are moments when it doesn't feel this way. If there is absolutely one thing you need reminded of right now as you grieve, it is that God has not forgotten you. He has not left you to figure out this grief on your own. He did not take a step back from your life and forget about you as you've faced all that you have. He is present with you, His heart grieves with yours, and He loves you. Know this right now. Cling to it. Don't forget it. We read this promise in Psalm 34:18. Remind yourself of this truth often:

The Lord is near the brokenhearted; he saves those crushed in spirit.
- **Psalm 34:18 (CSB)** [44]

Let's go back to Jeremiah's moment of remembering God's goodness and faithfulness in Lamentations 3.

<u>Yet</u> *I still dare to hope when I remember this: The faithful love of the Lord never ends! His mercies never cease. Great is his faithfulness; his mercies begin afresh each morning.*
-Lamentations 3:21-23 (NLT) [45]

God is faithful to you. He loves you. He is merciful toward you. He is faithful to you.

Here's what I want you to cling to. Our God is so personal, so close, and so desiring an intimate relationship with you that he knows your needs each day and his mercies for those differing daily needs will be new for you.

What your heart needs today is likely different from what your heart will need tomorrow. The day after that will have its own needs, and, well, you get the point. So each morning as you wake up, remember that as your heart is in need, ask Him for new mercy that day. He's going to be faithful to provide it and He will never hold back His mercies. He is SO good and SO loving and He desires for you to find all that you need in Him.

In what specific ways do you need God's mercy today? Write these out and begin to ask Him for mercy in these areas.

_____

_____

_____

_____

_____

In this chapter, we have been encouraged to "seek and find" and "taste and see that He is good." We need this constant reminder to do so because our grief and the difficult circumstances we face can blind us to the truth. The truth is that God is present and at work in our hearts and in our lives. That can be difficult to see or understand when our hearts ache.

So, turn back to these scriptures often to remind your heart of just how good, how loving, how faithful, how merciful, and how present He is. You may forget it at times throughout this tough season. Thank God for His presence with us as we endure hardship! This life is hard. This season of grief is unimaginably difficult. This heart of yours is overwhelmed.

Yet...

CHAPTER 6

FROM PEACE TO REJOICING

We all long for peace. I'd imagine that you would say your heart is in a place of unrest. Maybe you'd say you feel uneasy, overwhelmed, stressed, burdened, broken, and the list goes on. Remember back in Lamentations 3:17, when Jeremiah says, "Peace has been stripped away, and I have forgotten what prosperity is." And again in verses 19-20, when he says, "The thought of my suffering and homelessness is bitter beyond words. I will never forget this awful time, as I grieve over my loss."

His lack of peace in those moments is heartbreaking to even read. Not only does he feel that his peace has been stripped away, but he forgets what normal, good, enjoyable life looks like. His peace is so lacking that it has become a suffering that has led to extreme bitterness. Such suffering that he'll never forget this awful time. His heart was longing to find peace, and it was when he turned his heart and mind to the Lord, when he began to live in the "yet", he found it.

We all long for peace. What exactly does it mean to have peace?

Now, the world measures peace by what our circumstances look like. Are things going well? That's considered peaceful. Are my finances OK? Am I healthy? Are my kids acting the way I'd like? Well, then, life is peaceful. The world wants us to believe this is peace. But that's all circumstantial. So, if finances or health go awry, my heart no longer feels at peace. The world's idea of peace is bogus. God's peace is a peace that surpasses our understanding and is not dependent on circumstances. It surpasses all that the world would have us believe. It's a peace that comes from trusting Him.

And the peace of God, which surpasses all understanding, will guard your hearts and minds in Christ Jesus.
- **Philippians 4:7 (CSB)** [46]

This peace guards your heart. This peace also guards your mind. This peace protects you in the midst of hardship. It's the work of Christ in you that says, "No matter what you are enduring, it's going to be OK." Christ has the victory, so no matter what the Christian faces or must endure, we always know what and Who we have in Jesus. That allows our heart and mind to rest. This peace brings us rest when the world tells us we ought to feel overwhelmed and upset by our circumstances. This peace brings us rest when the world says life is not worth living. This peace brings us rest when the world says there is no hope. So how do we find that peace? We find it in God, even in the midst of the most difficult of circumstances.

5 *Rest in God alone, my soul, for my hope comes from him.*
6 *He alone is my rock and my salvation, my stronghold; I will not be shaken.*
7 *My salvation and glory depend on God, my strong rock. My refuge is in God.*
8 *Trust in him at all times, you people; pour out your hearts before him. God is our refuge.*
- **Psalm 62:5-8 (CSB)** [47]

Friend, He really is. He's a refuge you can rest in. He's a strong rock and because of His protection, you cannot and will not be shaken. He is trustworthy as a refuge, so, as we talked so much about earlier, pour out your heart to Him. With all this refuge talk, what exactly does it mean that God is our refuge? What is a refuge, anyway?

A refuge is a place of safety and protection in the midst of trouble. For the Christian, it's comfort in God's presence, knowing that no matter the circumstances, your heart is His.

It's easy to run to God for refuge when times are tough. It's even easier to go back to your normal day-to-day when things aren't so bad. God isn't calling us to run to Him when circumstances are difficult. He's calling us as Christians to hunker down in Him, find our refuge in Him, and not retreat from that place, ever. You see, God desires that we find all we need in Him and Him alone each moment of each day. And, when we live in the refuge that is Jesus, that's when the Holy Spirit truly changes our hearts. That's sanctification. That's growing in holiness. This is what He's called us to as those who have placed our faith in Him. Faith in Jesus is a daily, ongoing thing. It's not a one-time commitment and then going back to Him for help when times are tough. Jesus didn't call us to come-and-go with Him. Rather, He called us to remain in Him.

Why is this so important for you and I right now as we grieve? If we are coming and going, only running to His refuge in the midst of difficulty, we'll fail to seek refuge in Him because our emotions often rule the day when we aren't remaining in Jesus. So, what does this look like? I've watched friends seek to find refuge in alcohol, drugs, and those things that might take their mind off of their grief. I've encountered those who seek to find their refuge in solitude of their home, pushing away family, friends, and those seeking to walk alongside them in their grief. So many others turn to food, sexual encounters, frivolous spending and more. All as a response to their emotion and lack of peace, as they seek to find something, anything to ease those feelings. You see, when we don't remain in Jesus, we easily drift. Emotion leads us to drift from Jesus because we aren't thinking rightly in those moments. Grief is emotionally overwhelming, and we often aren't thinking rightly in the midst of it.

So, momentarily, we may FEEL like we have found a refuge in these things. Momentarily, these "places of refuge" keep us from dwelling on the loved one we lost. They may take the edge off of the deep hurt we feel. They may, for a bit, give us great pleasure or happiness, which hasn't been felt in a while. They may even, for a moment, make you feel normal again. Satan wants nothing more than for you to take your eyes off of Jesus in the midst of your grief to try and find a "refuge" that you think will give you the joy, peace, happiness, and normalcy you are longing for.

Refuge in Jesus each and every day is important. It's the most important thing. It's daily surrender to Him, finding all that you need in Him, and saying, "I can't do this life on my own. Jesus, it's yours". It's that moment of saying, "I'm incapable, Jesus, and I need you."

Think about this picture for a moment. A baby bird is hatched in the nest and it is 100% dependent on its parents. They bring it food, they keep it warm, and they protect it from predators. Over time, the baby bird grows feathers and keeps itself warm. It learns to fly and goes to find its own food. It learns how to protect itself and keep from harm. In time, this baby bird is an adult and can go off on it's own.

It would be pretty crazy to see a grown adult bird still sitting in the nest it was hatched in, wouldn't it? Imagine that same bird staying in the nest, desiring protection and food and warmth from its parents. You and I would say that this bird has its own life now, can do its own thing and be its own bird (person). Why would you depend so much on someone else when you can freely live your own life?

But there is an extreme difference between us and this bird. If we "leave the nest", there's danger beyond what we could ever imagine. More than that, there's separation from the Father, who desires that we remain with Him and He remains with us. So many fail to remember that He created us to be in relationship with us, and we so often feel like there has to be "more" outside the nest. In leaving, we lose all that He intended for us in His presence. He not only calls us to remain in Him, but to live in obedience and full surrender to Him as we remain there.

This is why Christianity is hated and misunderstood. We're called to deny ourselves and surrender fully to Him. Sure, we could live a life for ourselves. We're capable of it. But God calls us to live in the "nest", living completely surrendered to and dependent on Him. THIS is daily refuge in Jesus, finding all we need in Him. And, as we know to be true, He is absolutely faithful and trustworthy to those who surrender fully to Him. And, for those who know and love Jesus, you know that the "nest" isn't confinement. It's certainly not the lesser of the options. While the world says, "go, be you," you know that you have everything in Jesus and the world cannot compare to all you have in Him.

Grieving Christian, stay here with Him. Remain in His refuge. Live dependent on Him daily. Don't allow your emotions to lead you astray. You and I are prone to wander. Stay in Him. Stay with Him. And, when we do live in daily dependence on Him, His faithfulness will lead us to respond to Him in this way...

> **16** But I will sing of your strength and will joyfully proclaim
> your faithful love in the morning.
> For you have been a stronghold for me,
> a refuge in my day of trouble.
> **17** To you, my strength, I sing praises,
> because God is my stronghold—

my faithful God.
- **Psalm 59:16-17 (CSB)** [48]

How have you taken refuge in the Lord? How has He given you rest as you've trusted Him?

_____

_____

_____

_____

_____

In what other things have you sought to take refuge in? How did they fail to satisfy you in the ways only God can?

_____

_____

_____

_____

_____

Peace begins to take over our hearts when we come to this place of surrender that says, "I can't do this on my own. I'm going to trust you with this and find what I need in you as I rest in your presence." Peace begins to transform our hearts in the midst of grief. As the Spirit gives us His peace, we come to trust Him all the more.

You and I cannot find peace apart from Jesus. It's only when we look to Him and trust Him that He will provide our hearts peace. Only those who have placed their trust in Jesus can receive what the Holy Spirit gives. That kind of peace is only for the Christian. So, if you love Jesus and you are turning to Jesus, His Spirit is going to give your heart peace. Now, your heart may cling so fiercely to your circumstances that you are unable to accept that level of peace in the moment, but friend, He's offering it to you. We discussed this scripture earlier, but this is right here...

> We do not know what to do, but our eyes are on you.
> **-2 Chronicles 20:12, The MSG Translation** [49]

If you are going to receive the peace He is offering you, then you must turn to HIm. In your anger, your bitterness, your pain, and yes, even in your lack of peace like Jeremiah, turn to Him because you know that He has all you need. And the more your eyes are turned to Jesus, the more healing you are going to experience in your heart.

The deeper our trust in Jesus is, the more our hearts can respond to grief with, "I'm OK." That doesn't mean you can just move on. That doesn't mean you stop grieving. However, it means that you trust Jesus SO much in the midst of your grief that your hope in Him is even greater than the hurt in your heart. When you are in this place, you can respond to grief with, "my soul is OK because I have Jesus."

This is where Horatio Spafford found himself. In the midst of intense grief, he trusted the Lord to a degree that 150 years later, his words continue to be an incredible response of worship to the Lord. Mr. Spafford's name may not be familiar to you, but what he wrote may ring a bell.

Horatio Spafford lived in Chicago with his wife, Anna and five children. As a businessman in the city, he lost most of his business in the great Chicago fire of 1871. In that same year, their young son passed away with pneumonia. It wouldn't take much for you to feel what this man felt. To lose a dear loved one and then other difficult life circumstances hit. We've all been there. It's beyond overwhelming, isn't it?

Two years later, in 1873, while still fresh with the grief of losing their son, more tragedy hit. Horatio's wife and four daughters were on an ocean liner across the Atlantic toward Europe. Their ship collided with another in the middle of the Atlantic, killing 226, including all four of Horatio Spafford's children. Anna was pulled from the ocean as one of the low number of survivors.

Horatio Spafford found the next available ship in order to get to his wife, Anna. While across the Atlantic, the captain informed Horatio that they were over the spot where his children lost their lives. It was on that ship where Horatio Spafford penned the lyrics to "It Is Well With My Soul".

When peace like a river attendeth my way,
When sorrows like sea billows roll,
Whatever my lot, Thou hast taught me to say,
It is well, it is well with my soul.
Chorus:
It is well with my soul,
It is well, it is well with my soul [50]

Horatio Spafford was broken, hurting, and at a level of grief that I cannot begin to imagine. He'd lost a child two years prior and then lost four more. As we've spoken of often throughout this book, can you imagine his moments of asking God, "how?" How is this happening? How is it possible that I lose my 5 children? How am I supposed to go on with life?

While Mr. Spafford's grief was extreme, he never wavered in his focus on Jesus. That is apparent in the words he penned. No matter the grief, no matter the hurt, no matter the circumstances, it is well deep down in his soul. He knew of God's goodness, faithfulness, trustworthiness, mercy, and love. He knew the hope he had in Jesus. He knew what would lie ahead for him in glory. He had Jesus and that's all that mattered. So, the circumstances being what they were, his soul was still OK because of Jesus. He models living in the "yet" for us by trusting and rejoicing in the midst of his grief.

A HEART OF REJOICING

A heart at peace is a heart filled with hope. A heart filled with hope is a heart that rejoices. Let me just stop there for a moment. That word caught you, didn't it? Rejoice. How are we supposed to rejoice in the midst of the pain we feel? How can I rejoice when my heart continues to grieve? It can't be both ways, can it?

As we've talked about with other things, rejoicing isn't circumstantial. The rejoicing of the heart is an outflow of the peace we have because of Jesus. There's no stopping it. So, a heart that is trusting Jesus and living in the hope He gives, HAS to rejoice. It can't help but rejoice! And yes, a heart that is grieving can rejoice without dishonoring your loved one. So often, the grieving heart fails to rejoice because focus is placed on the circumstances instead of Jesus. The heart that is trusting Jesus will rejoice in all circumstances. And, know that this looks different for each person. Rejoicing doesn't always mean singing the Hallelujah Chorus at the top of your lungs as you walk down the street. Rejoicing is simply a posture of the heart that lives in thanks for what Christ has done on your behalf. It is not circumstantial. While you may have to be more intentional to rejoice in the midst of grief, it does not mean that grief robs you of the ability to rejoice in Jesus. The Christian rejoices because Christ has saved them. One who has been drug out of the depths of sin and given new life cannot help but live in thanks. For some, rejoicing is an outward expression. For others, it's not. But for all Christians, to rejoice is to remain in thankful joy because of who Jesus is and what He has done!

In the book of Habakkuk, the Prophet Habakkuk writes:

17 Even though the fig trees have no blossoms, and there are no grapes on the vines; even though the olive crop fails, and the fields lie empty and barren; even though the flocks die in the fields, and the cattle barns are empty, 18 yet I will rejoice in the Lord! I will be joyful in the God of my salvation! 19 The Sovereign Lord is my strength! He

*makes me as surefooted as a deer, able to tread
upon the heights.*
- **Habakkuk 3:17-19 (NLT)** [51]

Yet. There it is again. Even though times are tough. Even though my life is in shambles. Even though my heart is broken. Even though everything is falling apart around me, YET, I will still rejoice in the Lord!

Can you write this out in your own words? Give it a try, as hard as it may be...

Even though _____

Yet I will _____.

Friend, if you have not found yourself in this place, begin to ask the Lord to bring your heart there. Ask God to remind you of your salvation. Ask God to remind you of the cross. Ask God to remind you of how Christ has transformed your life. And as you remember these things, you are reminded of how good, how strong, how incredible He is. This can only lead to rejoicing. Another opportunity to turn back to God.

Even though _____ .....Yet, I will rejoice in the Lord!

I love how this text reminds me that it is all about Him. I don't personally have the strength to keep going as I grieve, and neither do you. But, He does. I don't have what it takes to step back into life. I don't have what it takes to keep going. On my own, I'm a mess. But, as I remain joyful in my salvation, I'm reminded that HE is my strength. He gives me the surefootedness of a deer, who even on uneven ground, can navigate and continue on without concern. So it is for our hearts as we trust Him. He is your strength. He is your guide. He is your everything. So, Christ-follower, rejoice in Him. It's quite alright to rejoice in worship with arms raised high while tears of hurt stream down your cheeks. It's just fine to give thanks to God as your heart continues to ache. That's the faith that God has called us to have. As we read earlier from Charles Spurgeon:

> "Tears are permitted, but they must glisten in the light of faith and hope."
> **-Charles Spurgeon** [52]

Jesus promised us that life would be difficult. You're experiencing that right now. But, he also promises us victory in Him, which is why we rejoice. He wins. We win.

> In this world you will have trouble. But take heart! I have overcome the world.
> **- John 16:33b (NIV)** [53]

There are better days ahead, friend. Because of Christ's life, death, and resurrection, those who have placed their trust in Him, those who love Him, will be with Him for eternity. As you grieve, take heart. Jesus wins. He is victorious and He has defeated death. Hell has no victory. The day you no longer hurt, no longer grieve, no longer feel broken, is coming.

> **3** *Then I heard a loud voice from the throne: Look, God's dwelling is with humanity, and he will live with them. They will be his peoples, and God himself will be with them and will be their God.* **4** *He will wipe away every tear from their eyes. Death will be no more; grief, crying, and pain will be no more, because the previous things have passed away.*
> **- Revelation 21:3-4 (CSB)** [54]

We rejoice because of Jesus. What He has done. What He is doing. What He will do. So, as you grieve, continue to turn your eyes to Jesus and worship Him.

There are so many reasons to be excited about Heaven. First and foremost for the Christian, is being with Jesus. What other specific things are you looking forward to in Glory?

_____

_____

_____

_____

_____

WORSHIP EVEN WHEN IT'S HARD

Years ago, Cathie and I endured a long and painful season of infertility. Four miscarriages, lost hope, intense grief, and a lot of questions. In that season, we sang a song at church in which the chorus spoke of God's goodness. I remember having a hard time giving voice to those words on the screen. I remember fighting through my desire to not sing. I remember thinking to myself, "is He?" Because of my confidence in who He is, even though I didn't understand how He'd allow this loss, I sang. I'd often think back to that first time hearing it as we battled infertility and the loss of our children. I would say those words to myself, speaking that praise to Him often as we endured that season. It's almost like my heart had to keep reminding my brain of how good He is.

A few years after first battling through this song, I received a call that would forever change our lives. When I said hello, the response was: "Tyler, we have two little boys for you." Our call came in and we had two little boys in Ethiopia who we'd just been matched with! I immediately drove to Cathie's office to tell her in person. In the car, for 25 minutes, I belted out those same words, rejoicing in his goodness. He is good. When times are hard and when circumstances have you feeling on top of the world. Rejoice in the hard and rejoice in the good, because of Jesus. Those lyrics were true when I sang them in the depths and when I sang them from the mountaintop. The truths of God don't change with our circumstances. He is good.

Psalm 40 is such an incredible chapter of rejoicing in the midst of grief and verse 1 was instrumental for me as we endured infertility and loss. While waiting patiently for the Lord, He sees and hears us. Those words are necessary to hear as we grieve. That truth is necessary for our hearts to cling to.

As difficult as life may seem and as broken as your heart may be, you and I can still praise God in the midst of it all. It's hard at times, I get it. However, the more time you spend seeking Him, the more time you are in His word, the more you are simply turned toward Him, your heart can't help but praise. Read Psalm 40 and allow the words to prompt your heart to rejoice in Him.

1 *I waited patiently for the Lord, and he turned to me and heard my cry for help.*
2 *He brought me up from a desolate pit, out of the muddy clay, and set my feet on a rock, making my steps secure.*
3 *He put a new song in my mouth, a hymn of praise to our God. Many will see and fear, and they will trust in the Lord.*
4 *How happy is anyone who has put his trust in the Lord and has not turned to the proud or to those who run after lies!*
5 *Lord my God, you have done many things—your wondrous works and your plans for us; none can compare with you. If I were to report and speak of them, they are more than can be told.*
6 *You do not delight in sacrifice and offering; you*

open my ears to listen. You do not ask for a whole burnt offering or a sin offering.

7 Then I said, "See, I have come; in the scroll it is written about me.

8 I delight to do your will, my God, and your instruction is deep within me."

9 I proclaim righteousness in the great assembly; see, I do not keep my mouth closed—as you know, Lord.

10 I did not hide your righteousness in my heart; I spoke about your faithfulness and salvation; I did not conceal your constant love and truth from the great assembly.

11 Lord, you do not withhold your compassion from me. Your constant love and truth will always guard me.

12 For troubles without number have surrounded me; my iniquities have overtaken me; I am unable to see. They are more than the hairs of my head, and my courage leaves me.

13 Lord, be pleased to rescue me; hurry to help me, Lord.

14 Let those who intend to take my life be disgraced and confounded. Let those who wish me harm be turned back and humiliated.

15 Let those who say to me, "Aha, aha!" be appalled because of their shame.

16 Let all who seek you rejoice and be glad in you; let those who love your salvation continually say,

"The Lord is great!"
17 I am oppressed and needy; may the Lord think
of me. You are my helper and my deliverer; my
God, do not delay.
   - **Psalm 40 (CSB)** [55]

Read through Psalm 40 again and write down all of the reasons you find to praise God in the midst of difficulty. What does Psalm 40 tell us about God's heart?

_____

_____

_____

_____

_____

What from Psalm 40 most led your heart to rejoice? Why? How can you remind yourself of this truth moving forward?

_____

_____

_____

_____

_____

Rejoicing might not be a daily thing for you right now. It might be something you have to work toward. It might be something you have to force yourself to do. But keep trusting Jesus and reminding yourself of His goodness. He will bring your heart to rejoice.

20 We put our hope in the Lord. He is our help and our shield. 21 In him our hearts rejoice, for we trust in his holy name. 22 Let your unfailing love surround us, Lord, for our hope is in you alone.

- **Psalm 33:20-22 (NLT)** [56]

CHAPTER 7

MOVING FORWARD IN THE YET

So now what? This truth and heart-shift to the "yet" from Lamentations 3 is life-changing, but only if we grab hold of it. Scratch that. Grabbing hold isn't strong enough language. We must cling to this as though our lives depend on it. Why? Because they do.

Think back with me to the movie "Twister." If you haven't seen it, I'm going to ruin it for you now that we are decades removed. Is it still a spoiler this far out? Spoiler alert: it's about people chasing tornados and we get to see a cow fly. That's pretty much it. They find tornadoes and drive toward them repeatedly. At the end of the movie, a tornado is bearing down and the only chance they have to survive is to hold tightly to a water pipe that is sticking out of the ground. This thing is anchored down so deep that there is no chance the tornado can uproot it. So, they run to this pipe, tie themselves to it, and hold on for dear life as the tornado passes over. They look up as they are in the eye of this thing, and as awful as the tornado was, they were OK. They clung tightly to the only thing that could save them. I don't know how realistic the scene is, but it's a great visual, so we're running with it. [57]

Friends, I pray that moving forward, this would be a picture of you. That in the middle of possibly the biggest storm you've ever endured, you are clinging tightly to Jesus. That as you look around the middle of this storm and see the lack of peace, the chaos in your heart, the missing hope, the sleepless nights, the extreme emotion and the deep hurt, that you would be reminded that you are safe in the Father's arms. And, from there, be able to stop and say, "and yet, God is good. And loving. And faithful. And merciful. I'm choosing to trust Him."

The last thing I would anticipate is that you'd close this book and feel any differently about your grief. I'd expect it to still be incredibly hard. However, I do hope that you soon close this book thinking, "God is faithful and I trust Him." He really is and you really can! As you continue to hurt (and you will), please keep seeking after and trusting Jesus. He's trustworthy and He WILL see you through this.

I'm sitting on the edge of a lake in the Smoky Mountains of east Tennessee as I write this chapter. It's absolutely beautiful here. In front of me, along the water line, is a sign that reads, *"Warning: This is not an approved swimming area. Swim at your own risk."*

Now, I don't know about you, but that isn't the most re-assuring thing to read. Why isn't it approved? What has happened here that you're not recommending that I take a swim? What monster lives under that water? Basically, what it sounds like they are trying to say (but couldn't fit it all on the sign) was, "This is a dangerous area to swim and it's out in the middle of nowhere. We really don't want you to do it and certainly wouldn't recommend it, but none of us are here to tell you not to and we can't tell you what to do, so...."

This is similar to our grief. There's a temptation to hole up and push away close relationships. A temptation to stop engaging with those you love and no longer enjoy the things you once did. The temptation to hide is real. It often feels better to do that, doesn't it? I won't argue that for a second. But, I also know that while it's OK to want to be alone for a while, it's certainly not healthy in the long-term. So, similar to that sign at the beach, I'm saying to you, *"This isolation is a dangerous place for you to be in for an extended time. I really don't want you to stay in this place and I certainly wouldn't recommend it, but I'm not there to tell you not to and I can't really tell you what to do, so...."*

Friend, I want what is best for you. I want to see you cared for, encouraged, lifted up, pointed to Jesus, and simply loved well by those in your life. That cannot happen when we close everyone off. Again, I get it. I've been there and it feels like the best place to be. I've said it before and I'll say it again, you and only you know when the right time is to step out and move forward in your grief. Move toward people, toward places, and toward some sort of normalcy. I'm not going to tell you that you have to do that right now and I'm not here to tell you when. But, as I just stated, I certainly wouldn't recommend staying isolated for a long period of time. It's difficult, awkward, and almost impossible to do at times, but work towards it. I cannot and will not tell you what to do, but I do want to encourage you in this way.

So what are some ways that you can move forward? Not move on, remember, just move forward, in trust. I'd like to give you a number of ways to move forward well in your relationships as you yourself live in the "yet". It is when we choose to live in the "yet" that we desire relationships and mutual encouragement the way that God created us to live in.

MOVE TOWARD YOUR FAMILY AND CLOSEST FRIENDS

When you are ready, take steps toward those you love most. Those you know will support, comfort and care for you well. Maybe that means attending a birthday party or family dinner. Maybe it's taking the step (or what feels like a giant leap) of attending a family Christmas. Holidays are hard, aren't they? You decide when your heart is ready to step back into those types of parties or get-togethers. Maybe it's as simple as inviting a friend to meet you for coffee. If your grief is fresh and you've holed yourself up, begin to write down things you can do once again with those you love that are comfortable for you and allow you to be in control.

What are 3 normal things you could do with your family or close friends that would help you take a step toward normalcy? Maybe it's a birthday party or holiday get-together? Maybe it's seeing a movie or grabbing coffee. Maybe it's going back to a specific club or group that you've met with for a long time. Write down 3 things that you'll take a step toward initiating in the coming days / weeks.

_____

_____

_____

_____

_____

What relationships have you distanced yourself from due to your grief? What steps can you take to move toward these people once again?

_____

_____

_____

_____

_____

I want to encourage you to move back toward those you've kept at arm's length. This can be difficult and awkward, especially if they were not there for you in your greatest times of need. Certainly, there are deep wounds created when someone you have been close to was not there when you needed them most. Many, while not knowing how to care for someone who is grieving, end up doing nothing. While you may have needed them in a big way, only to receive nothing, give them grace as you don't know all the information as to why. Either way though, it certainly cuts deep when those you love don't show up for you.

When Cathie's mom passed away, we watched as a number of those closest to us disappeared. We had a great need and desire for those we loved to be present with us.

Not a need for anything practical, but just for them to be. Instead, from many, it was...crickets. We experienced the same thing throughout our seasons of infertility and pregnancy loss with many who we thought were close friends. It was devastating. It was lonely. It was hurtful. When, at last, we felt like we could step back into relationships with both feet, it was hard because the first thing we wanted to say was, *"where were you? Where have you been? Why did you abandon us in our most difficult time?"*

Thankfully, there were others who stepped up and lived out 2 Corinthians 1:4, encouraging us, praying with us, making meals for us, and just being present. I know we are not alone in having experienced that kind of felt abandonment. If you have experienced that, I'm so sorry. We were designed to live in community, and so whether you pushed people away or others were simply not there for you, it's not a healthy way to grieve. While you may be wounded for those who have been absent, I'd encourage you to move toward them with grace and forgiveness. I get it, it's hard to do, but ask Jesus to do that work in your heart. He's faithful to do so.

I'd like you to take a step back toward your friends, family, and church family. Pursue relationships once again, not because it's easy, but because it's necessary. Allow others to love you, encourage you, challenge you, and point you to Jesus. Surround yourself again with those who you know will be what you need in this season.

GETTING RE-CONNECTED AT CHURCH

For some, this means returning to regular church attendance. For others, this means returning to those relationships within the church that you've disconnected from. For others, it's finally come time to give of yourself and serve your church family in some capacity. For some of you, all of these apply. Hear me that there is absolutely no judgment whatsoever if you have been disconnected relationally. Obviously, I'd love to hear that you had your people who persisted alongside you through this difficulty and who you remained connected to. But, grief will put up walls, drive you away from close relationships, and push you inward. It happens. That's not an excuse or crutch for us to use, so we have to fight this. God did not intend for us to ever do life alone or outside of community. Even more so, we are not designed to do grief alone or without community.

When it comes to attending church again, I know that can be overwhelming. It can feel like people are bombarding you, typically because they care, but it can still feel like the walls are coming in on you and you can't breath. It's a lot to face a number of people in the midst of grief, forcing you to rehash your emotions over and over again, oftentimes with people you don't even really trust with your emotions. If you have gotten yourself back to attending church, good for you. I also hope you are back to serving, but you take the time you need, if you still need it. If you have not gotten back into regular attendance at church, I'd like to suggest that it's time. I told you early in the book that I'd share some hard challenges with you, and I'd like to take this time to challenge you. It may feel easier to stay at home. It may feel overwhelming to put yourself out there again. It may feel like too much to have to face people and answer all the difficult questions you're sure they'll ask. But, please ask the Lord to give you what you need to take that step back toward your church family. He'll faithfully do just that and you'll be glad you took that step.

At the same time, you know your heart and mind better than anyone. If you just don't feel that you are ready, then take the time you need. Just be careful, as it is easy to fall into a routine of staying away from your church family to the point where it just feels more comfortable to stay home all the time. At a certain point, and you'll know when that is, you've got to push yourself to move forward back into relationships with friends, family, and church family. Let them be the comfort, encouragement and grace that they've been called to by the Lord. That's a humbling place to be, I get it, but let your church family love you. If you haven't already for someone else, you'd do the same for them. Allow the body of Christ to be used in your life.

BE A COMFORT TO OTHERS

No matter the stage of grief you are in or how long you have been grieving, I am confident that you have experienced God's comfort at some level. If you are a follower of

Christ, you've been comforted by the Father. We know this because it says so in 2 Corinthians 1....

> **3** *All praise to God, the Father of our Lord Jesus Christ. God is our merciful Father and the source of all comfort.* **4** *He comforts us in all our troubles...*
> - **2 Corinthians 1:3-4a (NLT)** [58]

How have you experienced God's comfort in the midst of your grief?

_____

_____

_____

_____

_____

As we grieve, it can be easy to take a break from anything missional. Being with people, as we just spoke about, is hard. Being with other grieving people is even more difficult, as the circumstances, emotions, and tears just bring it all flooding back from your own personal experience.

However, if you keep reading in 2 Corinthians 1, you'll see this in verse 4:

> **4** *He comforts us in all our troubles so that we can comfort others. When they are troubled, we will be able to give them the same comfort God has given us.* [59]

Now, you need to decide when you are ready to be available to others in their own grief. You may be reading and thinking, "no way, not yet", while you also may be saying, "It's time I make myself available to others, comforting them in their own grief." In your grief, you get to set boundaries. When you are ready, take advantage of the opportunities the Lord presents to you. There are many who will need you in the same way you've needed the love, comfort and encouragement of others.

I know a family who lost their teenage son after a lengthy battle with an ugly disease. Obviously heartbroken, this family grieved hard over the loss of their son. Not long after, another family in the church lost their teenage son who had been battling cancer for almost 10 years. I watched as the first family took the second family under their wings. They showed up big. They had been there, they understood, and they made themselves available. They lived out 2 Corinthians 1:4 in a huge way. I'll never forget how cool this was to watch from the front row. If you haven't already been this for someone, your time is coming and I'm excited for the comfort you will be to another hurting person.

Who has comforted you well in the midst of your grief? What did they do / say? What about their comfort and presence did you most appreciate?

_____

_____

_____

_____

_____

If / When you are ready, who might you be able to comfort in the near future? What steps can you take to prepare your heart to do this?

_____

_____

_____

_____

_____

HOLDING OTHERS UP

On a chilly February day in Nashville, I was on my commute home from the office. As I took a big curve off of one highway and onto another, I slammed on the brakes and came screeching to a halt. There, sitting on a slope off the road was a pickup truck on its side. It had flipped, smashed into a wall of rock, and was now laying on its driver's side. I jumped out of my car and ran to this truck, meeting about 5 other men who had also stopped to help. When we got there, we quickly realized that this truck was about to tip over onto it's top. The man inside was badly injured and was saying things that led us to believe that he had sustained some level of head trauma. I'm certainly no doctor, but I knew he was injured to a degree that he could not afford to have his truck roll again while he was trapped inside.

While we had been evaluating the situation, a few more had stopped to help. Nobody was in a position to pull him out and help him, and even if we wanted to, that would require breaking the windshield to get in, which could further injure this man. Taking care of his medical needs was for the professionals to do. Our job in that moment was to keep that truck from rolling over on this small hill it was teetering on. So the 8 of us placed both hands on the top of his truck, dug our heels in, and braced ourselves there. We were determined that this truck was not rolling on our watch. During that time, we held this man up and took turns speaking to and encouraging him. It took 15 minutes for help to arrive, and when they did, they immediately put up large metal jacks in our place. This kept the truck from rolling so that they could tend to this man without any concern.

Why do I tell you this story? There was a man in a dire position and his circumstances were extreme. It was not our job to fix him. However, what were we able to do? We could hold him up and encourage him. So, that's what we did. We didn't try to do more than what we knew needed to be done in the moment. We simply lifted up a brother who was not able to help himself during a difficult situation.

I want you to keep this visual in mind as you move forward. You have been that person in need with a team who lifted you up and encouraged you. You know what it's like for things to look bleak on your end while others selflessly cared for you, propped you up, and comforted you through a difficult season. Think often about this visual, both of those who lifted you up and who you may have the opportunity to prop up and encourage in the future.

As you continue on in your own grief, you are going to have opportunities to comfort others in the way God has comforted you. God isn't calling you to fix or heal anyone of their grief. He isn't calling you to give them peace. He'll do that. He's simply calling you to hold others up by being an encouragement and comfort, just as our group of strangers did with a man we knew needed us in that moment. You have an opportunity to walk alongside, comfort, and point others to Jesus who are walking a similar journey as you have (or still are).

In my years as a Care Pastor, we offered GriefShare groups at our church. As you're probably aware, finding volunteers to lead a grief ministry is not an easy task. However, I happened to strike gold with a team that effectively led this ministry for a number of years. We had a couple who had lost their teenage daughter a few years prior. We had a couple who had lost their college-aged son 20 years prior. We had a widow who lost her husband about 15 years prior and a woman in her late 70s who was very newly widowed. Every single member of this team initially pushed back when I asked them to consider the opportunity. They weren't sure if they were ready. They weren't sure if they could do it emotionally. They weren't confident in their ability to help other grieving hearts. But, they allowed the Lord to use them and did He ever use them! Lives were changed! Unbelievers came to the group and found Jesus because of the hope they witnessed in those leaders.

This team would be the first to admit, and I'll say it as well. They didn't do anything special. Here's what they did. They trusted Jesus to give them the words and opportunities with others who were grieving. Then, when those opportunities arose, they used their own grief experiences and their own story of faith and they introduced people to the One who offers peace and hope that can be found nowhere else. Going back to the story I just shared, they held up and encouraged those who were broken and desperate for someone to walk alongside them in their grief. Was it worth it? Absolutely. Was it easy? If we are being honest, no, it wasn't easy at all. Their own grief was brought up often. A lot of old wounds were opened up. A lot of emotions resurfaced. Not easy at all. Really difficult, actually! They would all tell you though that it was worth it because people who were hopeless, found hope. Those who were without peace, found peace. Those who didn't know Jesus, found Jesus. Worth it. Absolutely stinking worth it! There is redemption seeping out of these stories and it jacks me up just to think about grieving people selflessly loving, serving and comforting other grieving people. This is what happens when people choose to live in the "yet", and it's amazing!

The timing of this is up to you, but don't run from the opportunity. Just as those who have grieved were a comfort and support to you, at a certain time, you can and should be that to others. If you haven't already, begin to ask God when your heart is ready and ask Him to give you what you need to do so. Ask Him for the strength to lift up and encourage those who are grieving. Whether it's in a group setting, sitting in the home of a family who just lost a loved one, or having coffee with someone who is freshly walking the journey you've been on for some time, you have an incredible opportunity. As someone who loves Jesus and has lost much, point people to the hope you have in Jesus. You may be experiencing grief, but Jesus' command to you and I to go and make disciples still stands.

SHARE YOUR HOPE WITH OTHERS

You've heard the testimonies of a number of folks through-out this book who have trusted Jesus through extreme grief. A common theme you'll see here is that although they are grieved to their core, their hope in Jesus remains. Friends, as pained as you may be, keep in mind as a follower of Jesus that you have incredible gospel opportunities with those who are grieving, and yet, have nothing to cling to. No hope, whatsoever. They haven't gotten to the "Yet", be-cause, for them, there is no "Yet". They are stuck in the no hope, no peace, misery that is life without Jesus.

Fortunately for you, although you've experienced the worst grief has to offer, you've been able to say, "Yet, God is loving, merciful, and faithful." You've trusted the creator of the universe and He's been faithful to you. You've tasted and seen that the Lord is good. As Jesus commands, remain there, finding all that you need in Him. He'll continue to be faithful to you.

There are others who have not experienced the grace that God has to offer. If that is you, if you have read through this book without having responded to the gospel, I am so thankful that you've done so. If you have not yet placed your trust in Jesus, but are interested in knowing more, praise Jesus! Auger into the following truths and respond to Jesus!

1. God is the perfect creator of all things.
2. All people sin and are separated from God because of it.
3. God provided us a way out by sacrificing His perfect Son, Jesus Christ, to pay the penalty of our sin.
4. Jesus lived a perfect life and He died on the cross for your sin. He raised from the dead and has prepared a place in Heaven with Him for those who love Him.
5. We respond to the work of Jesus by trusting Him and acknowledging that through He alone can we be saved. This response is a turning from sin and to God.

If this trusting Jesus thing is new to you, find someone to disciple you and point you to Jesus. If you need a resource, I had the privilege of leading a team at LifeWay Christian Resources that created the book, *My New Life: A New Christian's Guide to Building Your Life on God's Word.* Get your hands on this and allow a foundation to be built for your new life in Jesus! Or, if you've been a Christian and you would love a refresher on what life in Jesus looks like, this would be a great resource!

CLOSING

It's an honor to have walked a short season of your grief journey with you. Although I wasn't personally there as you read, know that I take seriously the opportunity to share these truths with you. And, as I said earlier, I hope to one day hear your story and how God has proved Himself faithful and drawn you nearer to His heart because of it. If you are interested in reaching out to me, you can do so by emailing me at **theyetbook@gmail.com** or finding me on Instagram **@TylerQuillet**.

I am so sorry for your loss. I truly am. My heart breaks for the hurt and pain your heart has endured. I know all too well the feelings of loss and the lack of peace, the bitterness, and the hopelessness that comes along with it. I also know the incredible peace that our Lord and Savior, Jesus Christ, gives us. I am overwhelmed daily with hope because of who He is and what He has done. My grief remains and I'm working through it today, and, most likely until my time on earth here is done. It's living in that beautiful place called "Yet," where we find ourselves grieving and, only because of Jesus, full of hope. May you find yourself in that place now until the day you see Jesus face to face, where he will wipe every tear from your eyes and there will be no more grief, no more pain, no more loneliness, no more hopelessness, no more bitterness, and no more lacking in peace. We'll have Jesus and it will be perfect.

I pray that in this season, He would draw you nearer to Himself, make you more like Himself, and bring Himself glory through you. I pray that the response of your broken heart would be one of trust that brings God glory. I pray that people would come to know Jesus in a personal way because they witnessed your deep trust in Him through great loss. I pray that you would be comforted by the One who is most faithful, most present, most merciful, gracious, and loving.

Once more, be reminded of what living in the "Yet" looks like, from Jeremiah's example. Grieve as you need, and know that you'll never forget this awful time. And yet, as always, the Lord is faithful, He is merciful, and He is good. You are loved and He is present with you during this time. Be reminded of these truths as you grieve and cling tightly to Him moving forward.

> **17** Peace has been stripped away, and I have forgotten what prosperity is.
> **18** I cry out, "My splendor is gone! Everything I had hoped for from the Lord is lost!"
> **19** The thought of my suffering and homelessness is bitter beyond words.
> **20** I will never forget this awful time, as I grieve over my loss.
> **21 Yet** I still dare to hope when I remember this:
> **22** The faithful love of the Lord never ends! His mercies never cease.
> **23** Great is his faithfulness; his mercies begin afresh each morning.
> **24** I say to myself, "The Lord is my inheritance; therefore, I will hope in him!"
> **25** The Lord is good to those who depend on him, to those who search for him.
> - **Lamentations 3:17-25 (NLT)** [60]

I don't have a big charge for you in closing. No locker

room speech to send you out. My desire is that your heart is seeking after and trusting Jesus more now than when you opened this book. More than that, I truly hope, as I said earlier, that you have gone from...

> I have Jesus, but I'm completely overwhelmed by grief.

to

> I have grief, but I'm completely overwhelmed by Jesus.

May you close this book and turn to Jesus today, tomorrow, and every day beyond that you are blessed with. As you do, these scriptures are my prayer over you.

> **24** 'May the Lord bless you and protect you. **25** May the Lord smile on you and be gracious to you. **26** May the Lord show you his favor and give you his peace.'
> **-Numbers 6:24-26 (NLT)** [61]

> **13** I pray that God, the source of hope, will fill you completely with joy and peace because you trust in him. Then you will overflow with confident hope through the power of the Holy Spirit.
> **-Romans 15:13 (NLT)** [62]

YET

May you, as you grieve the loss of those you so dearly love, be overwhelmed by the presence of Jesus...

ENDNOTES

PRE-FOREWORD

1. John Piper, "**Letter to a Parent Grieving the Loss of a Child**," Desiring God, April 22, 2013, https://www.desiringgod.org/articles/letter-to-a-parent-grieving-the-loss-of-a-child.

INTRO

2. Lam 3:17-24 (New Living Translation)

CHAPTER 1

3. David Sonnenschein, **Sound Design: The Expressive Power of Music, Voice and Sound Effects in Cinema** (Michael Wiese Productions, 2001).
- With personal permission from originator of quote, Gary Rydstrom.

4. Introduction to the book of Lamentations, **HCSB Study Bible: Holman Christian Standard Bible**. Nashville, TN: Holman Bible Publishers, 2010. 1333-1337.

5. Introduction to the book of Lamentations, **HCSB Study Bible: Holman Christian Standard Bible**. Nashville, TN: Holman Bible Publishers, 2010. 1333-1337.

6. Lam 3:19-24 (New Living Translation)

7. Jn 11:35 (Christian Standard Bible)

8. Ps 119:28 (Christian Standard Bible)

CHAPTER 2

9. Ps 13:1-3 (New Living Translation)

10. Ps 22:1-2 (New Living Translation)

11. Ps 42:3-5 (New Living Translation)

12. Ps 73:13-14 (New Living Translation)

13. Ps 10:1 (New Living Translation)

14. Ps 69:1-3 (New Living Translation)

15. Sally Breedlove, **Choosing Rest: Cultivating a Sunday Heart in a Monday World** (NavPress, 2002), 113-114.

16. Lam 3:17-20 (New Living Translation)

17. Zeph 3:17 (Christian Standard Bible)

18. Is 41:10, (Christian Standard Bible)

19. Jonathan Evans, Memorial Service for Dr. Lois Evans (Eulogy, Dallas, TX, January 6, 2020).

20. Is 55:8 (Christian Standard Bible)

CHAPTER 3

21. Lam 3:21-24 (New Living Translation)
22. D. Martyn Lloyd-Jones, **Spiritual Depression: Its Causes and Cures,** (Eerdmans; Reprinted edition, 1965), pp. 20-21.
23. 2 Chron 20:12 (The Message Translation)
24. Helen Howard Lemmel, **Turn Your Eyes Upon Jesus**, 1922.

CHAPTER 4

25. Music by Elevation Worship Publishing, "**Do it Again**", Recorded on September 9-21, 2016, track #2 on **Speak Revival** (Provident Label Group, 2017)
26. John Piper, "**What is Hope?**," Desiring God, April 6, 1986, https://www.desiringgod.org/messages/what-is-hope
27. Lam 3:21 (New Living Translation)
28. Lam 3:24 (New Living Translation)
29. Rev 21:4 (Christian Standard Bible)
30. Rom 8:18 (Christian Standard Bible)
31. Jn 14:2-4 (Christian Standard Bible)
32. Rev 22:12a (Christian Standard Bible)
33. Rom 5:2-5 (New Living Translation)
34. Rev 21:3-4 (New Living Translation)
35. Richard Rolheiser, **Sacred Fire: A Vision For a Deeper Human and Christian Maturity** (Image, 2014), 309-310.
36. C.H. Spurgeon, **Beside Still Waters: Words of Comfort for the Soul**, ed. Roy H. Clarke (Thomas Nelson, 1999), 235.

CHAPTER 5

37. Jer 29:12-14a (New Living Translation)
38. 2 Chron 20:12 (The Message Translation)
39. Ps 34:4-8, 17-18 (New Living Translation)
40. Ps 34:5 (New Living Translation)
41. Is 41:10 (New Living Translation)
42. 2 Chron 20:12 (The Message Translation)
43. Zeph 3:17 (Christian Standard Bible)
44. Ps 34:18 (Christian Standard Bible)
45. Lam 3:21-23 (New Living Translation)

CHAPTER 6

46. Phil 4:7 (Christian Standard Bible)
47. Ps 62:5-8 (Christian Standard Bible)
48. Ps 59:16-17 (Christian Standard Bible)
49. 2 Chron 20:12 (The Message Translation)
50. Spafford, Horatio. "It Is Well with My Soul." 1876. In **The Baptist Hymnal**, edited by Wesley L. Forbes, hymn 410. Nashville, TN: Convention Press, 1991.
51. Hab 3:17-19 (New Living Translation)
52. C.H. Spurgeon, **Beside Still Waters: Words of Comfort for the Soul**, ed. Roy H. Clarke (Thomas Nelson, 1999), 235.
53. Jn 16:33b (New International Version)
54. Rev 21:3-4 (Christian Standard Bible)

55. Ps 40 (Christian Standard Bible)
56. Ps 33:20-22 (New Living Translation)

CHAPTER 7

57. **Twister**. Directed by Jan de Bont. Written by Michael Chrichton and Anne-Marie Martin. N.P., Amblin Entertainment, 1996.
58. 2 Cor 1:3-4a (New Living Translation)
59. 2 Cor 1:4 (New Living Translation)
60. Lam 3:17-25 (New Living Translation)
61. Num 6:24-26 (New Living Translation)
62. Rom 15:13 (New Living Translation)

Made in the USA
Coppell, TX
08 July 2020